Secrets
of the Most
Holy Place

Secrets of the Most Holy Place

by Don Nori

Destiny Image® Publishers, Inc.
P.O. Box 310
Shippensburg, PA 17257-0310

"We Publish the Prophets"

ISBN 1-56043-076-1

For Worldwide Distribution
Printed in the U.S.A.

Seventh Printing: 1998   Eighth Printing: 1999

This book and all other Destiny Image, Revival Press,
and Treasure House books are available
at Christian bookstores and distributors worldwide.

For a U.S. bookstore nearest you, call **1-800-722-6774**.
For more information on foreign distributors,
call **717-532-3040**.
Or reach us on the Internet: **http://www.reapernet.com**

iv

Dedication

To Dick Woodcock,
a true mentor, leader and friend.
He is a man of honor and integrity.

Ministerial Outreach

Don Nori ministers on a limited basis to national and international conferences as his schedule permits. If you wish to inquire about Pastor Nori's ministry, or would like itinerary information, please call Destiny Image Publishers at 717-532-3040.

Please be sure to place the phase "personal correspondence" on all written correspondence, and address your inquiry to:

Pastor Don Nori
Destiny Image Publishers
P.O. Box 310
Shippensburg, PA 17257

Contents

Foreword

Here is an exhilarating, exciting book.

I can think of no greater need than to see expressed the truth of Jesus Christ in fresh new ways. If there is any part of the gospel that needs such a new expression, it is that which deals with the deeper aspects of Jesus Christ. Don has done us a great service of touching, in bright new ways, these profound truths.

This work goes beyond mere theological exegesis to touch the heart of the Lord. Searching this book for theology will not suffice; allow it to lead you deep into the realm of relationship with Jesus.

We will never know a subject greater than the much neglected subject of our oneness with Jesus Christ. Don takes you, in a living and dynamic way, into the veil and beyond the veil where blurs the line between things earthly and things divine. You will find in these pages a new appreciation of warfare, of prayer, of the Christian "in" Christ and of that Christian being lost in his union with his Lord.

Nor does Don end there, but he takes us on to the battlefield...that of our inheritance. He gives us a new hunger for the Church and brilliantly shows us that our inheritance and Christian community are now and not for some future millennial age.

This book is not a statement of doctrine or theology. It is an experience with God, a wonderful, dynamic journey that can lead you beyond the traditional realms of Christianity.

If you take his words to heart, you will experience them.

Gene Edwards, Author
Lewiston, Maine
January 29, 1992

Introduction:
You Are Expecting
to Hear from the Lord

You are expecting to hear the voice of the Father from within the veil. Your heart is open and your ear is tuned to Him who has much to say to mankind. You will not be satisfied merely to look on as He beckons a nation of priests to enter the veil.

And He is beckoning. He is calling a priesthood to Himself, a priesthood in which you can participate. Far beyond the voice of the prophet, deep in the heart of God, is His desire for you to be like Jesus. By your lifestyle, your voice and your ministry, you point to the Lord Jesus, seated with the Father within the veil.

Beyond the clamor and bustle of today's prophecy rises the crescendo of the sound of a trumpet, as part of an orchestra tuning before a great concert. You are part of this priesthood. You are in key and tuned to Him. Together with His Church, you are producing a new sound in the earth. This is not like the old sound. It is brand new, and it calls to you to put an end to your busyness, to your many activities, and to listen to the voice of the Lord. Only then will your activities become His activities, producing gold and silver rather than the wood, hay and stubble of a stubborn church building her own kingdom.

You are expecting to hear from the Lord. You are expecting to hear the secrets of the Most Holy Place. "The secret of the Lord is for those who fear Him, and He will show them His covenant." His secret is not for the proud or the self-assured. It is not for show or for profit; it is for Him and Him alone. It is through Him and Him alone. It is in Him and Him alone. It is for you. And His invitation is extended to you. As you walk through the pages of this book, allow yourself to respond to this invitation and discover its wonderful depths.

But there is a new sound in the earth. Slow down. No, stop! Listen! As a breeze lightly brushes a meadow in autumn, ushering in a distinct change in the weather, so the Spirit of the Lord is brushing the Church. He is gaining her attention, gaining your attention. Quietly does He convince her, convince you, deep within, that a distinct change is at hand.

Don't be misled by the lightness of the breeze, for its gentleness is deceptive; it ushers in the greatest spiritual upheaval of all time. The prophetic weather vane has turned. The Holy Spirit is blowing into the Holiest Place of all, ever drawing His people in, ever drawing you to a Place where there is no duality, no distraction, no competition. But there, within the veil, is He alone, ever calling you, "Come up hither."

You are beginning a journey, one that you have never traveled before. It is without question the most thrilling, yet most dangerous, pilgrimage of all, for it will surely cost you your life as you know it. You stand at the torn veil, your heart burning for Him, peering into the age to come and realizing that you are on the threshold of His Day.

The baggage of religious trappings must be dropped at the rent veil, for as you enter, you enter alone: You may bring no credentials, no titles, no gifts. Only His Light covers your nakedness and His Presence gives you strength. For this is His Domain, this is His Territory. Man only participates in this realm in response to a God who needs not his counsel, his strength or his wit. He can do it all on His own. He only chooses to work through you because He loves you so totally.

The Wind of the Spirit turns your heart toward God's eternal purposes, revealing that we are between two days. The imperfect is giving way to the perfect; the child is giving way to the man; the partial is giving way to fulness; dimness is giving way to un-approachable light as His glory shines in the face of Jesus Christ. You are about to know as you are known. Faith and hope, attributes of future anticipation, are giving way to love, the present fulfillment of yesterday's dream and tomorrow's hope. Today is the day of salvation, the unveiling of the New Covenant in all its fulness.

The Holy Spirit continues to stir you; you begin to discover your ministry within the veil and His permanent station on the Mercy Seat, from which you are invited to rule and reign with Him. As He comes again, He returns not as a sin-bearer, but as He who reveals and administrates the fulness of the New Covenant to hungry and expectant hearts.

Finally, but most preciously, the Spirit lays open your heart and you hear the rapturous word of the Lord: "When we see Him, we will be like Him, for we shall see Him as He is." Salvation is beginning to manifest; you are about to see Jesus as never before. In all His holiness, all His convincing splendor, you will see Him: In the twinkling of an eye, when you see Him you are changed—you are like Him. For the King, whom you serve, is suddenly coming to His Temple.

This is one time man cannot fake an experience with God. This One proceeds from His throne, flowing, gushing forth from the Most Holy Place like a mighty river. It is neither man-initiated nor man-completed. This does not smell of the sweat of humanity because man has no part but to be there and let God be God, literally, totally and without reservation.

The sound of your shouts, rebukes and demonizing warfare quiet as you move within the veil. There, all man's spiritual battles are consumed by the awesome reality of His final victory. As you take your seat with Jesus, you are stunned at the revelation of the defeated enemy. Instead of the shout of war, there is the shout of a conqueror, the shout of worship and a song of intimacy welling up in your heart. Who can but praise the Lord? Who can but acknowledge His might?

You are expecting to hear from the Lord. His promise is firm. He fulfills it without a hint of regret. Rather, to bring it about is the joy of His heart. All who hear, all who respond, will be intimately seated with Him within the veil. I know you will find the fulfillment of your heart's desire. I know you are one of these people. Your heart gives you away.

Chapter One

The Secret
of the Most
Holy Place

There is a secret. It is the secret of the Most Holy Place, where God alone dwells. To be sure, He has always wanted you to share the glory of His Presence and His majesty. He has prepared the Most Holy Place as a place of fellowship and ministry for you who are being drawn to this most wonderful realm of life. As you see Him in this realm, your fellowship and your ministry toward Him are on the highest plateau of experience possible this side of eternity. God has always wanted this. He planned it. He ordained it.

This is so vastly different than what you have been taught all your Christian life. Christianity had always been steeped in future hope, but seemed to contain very little present reality. Tomorrow would be better. In Heaven you would see the Lord. You would have to die to experience release from pain and suffering. Most of what Jesus died for was relegated to some future time. The only thing the cross purchased on this side was the assurance of eternal life with God after death.

Such a religion, of course, offers little hope for the present. It offers few answers to the intense difficulties of this life, and leaves your faith irrelevant to present reality and circumstance. Locking up the Kingdom for Heaven, you are left on your own to battle through this life.

There is never hope for today in this kind of religion, never hope for a better life now—only a whimsical promise that someday, over on the other side, things would be different, things would be better. "Over there," Jesus would wipe away every tear, every sorrow and every pain. "Over there" was no despair, no suffering and no fear.

Certainly, this does not imply that Heaven does not offer these wonderful benefits. To be sure, it does. Jesus' death and resurrection have provided an eternity free from those troubles that have kept you sorrowful for years. Certainly in Heaven there will be joy unspeakable. Certainly in Heaven there will be health and wholeness. Certainly in Heaven there will be knowledge and understanding.

But listen carefully. The purpose of Jesus' coming to earth was to bring Heaven's experience to earth. The wholeness and health of Heaven was to come to you. The rule of God, the Lordship of Jesus Christ in Heaven, was intended to be an experience, not just in Heaven after death, but of life right here on earth.

That is why, when the disciples asked Jesus to teach them to pray, He taught them to say, "Thy Kingdom come. Thy will be done, on earth as it is in Heaven." As God's will was always being performed in Heaven, His plan was, and still is, for His will to be fulfilled in your heart. Union and wholeness are available in the Person of God Himself in this life.

Jesus did not come just so you could go to Heaven. He did not come only to offer a future hope. Jesus did not even come merely to answer meager prayers for help and safety. He came so that you might experience the fulness of God, as well as all Heaven has to offer, so that His Kingdom could be established in the earth...starting within you.

The Church has barely begun to experience or to understand what all this means. She is so caught up in the struggles of this life that she cannot begin to comprehend the vastness of God's power and the totality of His plan for the human race in this life. The Church has underestimated His power and His ability. She has been unwilling to understand how much more powerful and loving He is than she has ever dreamed possible.

God is not just for Heaven anymore. In fact, He never was just for Heaven. He is for the here and now. He is, as always, inviting you to dwell with Him, in the sweetness and fulness of His manifest Presence within the veil of the Most Holy Place. Then, at last, His Kingdom will be established in the earth.

Chapter Two

The Secret
of First
Corinthians 13

B efore you begin your journey, we need to be sure you are ready for what you are about to experience. Like a mountain climber who checks his maps and charts to be sure he understands the climb ahead, you must be familiar with the territory to be explored. You are, however, at a slight disadvantage: Not many have explored this land before, so the way is virtually uncharted. We have only occasional reports from those who have been there, but we will do our best to prepare you. Nonetheless, you must be ready for the unexpected, for when you explore God's Domain, the unexpected is usually the rule of the day.

There is a secret locked in First Corinthians chapter 13. The secret is a portal of transition between two eras, two ages. Here, the apostle stretches back into the Holy Place, reaching for those whose hearts yearn after the Lord's. He gently draws them from one age to the next, preparing these saints to experience God in a dimension so far ahead of them that most will not ever realize what He has done. He gives a brief glimpse into the unfathomable realm of His fulness that, once experienced, forever becomes the quest of him who enters.

The Corinthians were not much different than most churches, muttering around the Holy Place, stumbling over various issues and excelling in others. The gift realm is the realm of duality; flesh cannot be avoided there. You can hear the apostle trying to explain spiritual realities to this typical church. With the partial light of the Holy Place, a light created only by the candlesticks of the Spirit, he explains how various gifts can be at work in a singular, yet many-membered, body. He speaks of prophecy and of tongues, of confusion and of order. He is trying to maintain a delicate balance between each truth, being painfully aware of the church's carnality and, thus, the obvious tendencies toward legalism, formulas and seeking opportunity for selfish gain.

With an air almost of exasperation, Paul halts his discourse as the scribe frantically writes his words. The apostle waves his hands, saying, "Hold it, all this is so technical. Let me show you a more excellent way!" Paul begins to unveil the fulness of God within the veil to these confused, albeit honest, brethren. He draws them back to the precious divine motivation behind every gift, every ministry and every unction of the Spirit, the love of God. He puts their activity on trial as he forces them to discern their motivations and their goals.

Paul writes to them in a way reminiscent of Jesus' conversation when He said, "Many will come to Me in that day and say, 'Lord, Lord, did we not prophesy in Your Name, and in Your Name cast out demons? Did we not do many mighty works in Your Name?' And I will answer them, 'I never knew you; depart from Me, you who practice lawlessness.' " There is no pure motivation apart from genuine relationship. Genuine relationship is born and nurtured as the fulness of the New Covenant is experienced. The New Covenant is experienced where the blood is sprinkled. The blood is sprinkled on the Mercy Seat, and the Mercy Seat is within the veil.

Paul knows that the only real hope for the Church, the only real hope for you and I, lies within the veil. He begins to show that the outward expressions of the Spirit-filled life have significance only if they are the result of deep inner relationship with Jesus and of a continuous, genuine heart change. He flatly states, with no apologies, that the gift of tongues means nothing in itself, even though he testified that he himself avidly prayed in tongues. The things these early Corinthians enjoyed would eventually cease: prophecy, tongues and knowledge.

But there is a greater realm of experience and power that is currently being missed. This "greater realm" is that of completeness or fulness. Paul agitates the Corinthians with his insinuations that there is more than what they have experienced. In effect, he is saying that they will never touch the fulness of God's plan of redemption if they are mired along the way.

Clearly, the gift realm is an experience "along the way," not the full expression of God's heart. Paul exhorts the church to abandon the fleshly realm, the partial, and to go on to perfection. He forces them to see where they are—in childhood! The key is to lay childish things behind, the things of the partial, the gift realm, and to go on to manhood or fulness.

Remember the layout of the Temple? The Outer Court corresponds to the initial conversion experience and gives entry into the Holy Place. In this second court, the candlesticks, oil and flame correspond to a humanity filled with the Holy Spirit. The Outer Court experience, while giving you eternal life, offers no spiritual light; it is illumined only by the light of the natural sun. In the Holy Place, flesh and spirit work together to produce light. This realm of mixture is the realm of the partial, the child, the imperfect, the dark mirror.

Within the veil, however, there is no mixture. This is the realm of "all Him." Within the veil, the work of man is not permitted. Within the veil, the sweat of man has no place. For there, God alone is preeminent. There God initiates.

The realm within the veil is all Spirit. Whatever you see there, you see by the light of God. There is no natural sun, there are no burning candlesticks. There is, however, the unapproachable light of His Presence shining and pulsating from between the cherubim above the Mercy Seat. In this realm is light and mercy. There is no warfare, no sickness and no pain. Within the veil, there is the perfect, the Man, the fulness. Within the veil is the Lord alone.

In the realm of the partial, the Holy Place, abide faith and hope; but in the Most Holy Place, love abides. Faith and hope cause you to look forward to that which you have not yet attained. Love is a *now* experience. It describes the greatest encounter, the present reality: His love shining in and filling your heart with Himself.

So with your heart crying out for Him, it's time to begin your journey. The fans of anticipation excite that fire deep within. Remember, those who seek, find. You are finding Him in all His glorious splendor.

Chapter Three

The Secret
of
Unapproachable
Light

You have the power to approach Him who is unapproachable. You are equipped to stand within the veil, looking intently between the cherubim above the Seat of Mercy. There is no room for the haughty within the veil. There is no room for the one who boasts of his achievements, his giftings or his talents. But there is room for the one who truly seeks Him. I know you are one person who wants Him. Your heart gives you away.

You want Him! Your heart aches for fellowship and intimacy with Him. Little else gives the joy and fulfillment that He gives. Precious little else gives you a reason to live.

So your heart drives you to search for His nearness and His tenderness. You are compelled by your telltale heart, one that won't be satisfied with anything less than Him, to diligently search for Him. So you walk around the Temple, gently and lovingly touching its structure, yearning for more, yearning for Him.

In your search for Him, you find the entrance and pass the laver of the Outer Court to find yourself standing in the light of the candlesticks of the Holy Place. But for all the joy and inner satisfaction that this brings, you are almost forced, by a power greater than yourself—His love—to press even further.

Your thoughts linger on the curtains that separate you from the Most Holy Place, where God Himself dwells. You pace back and forth along this forboding veil. You are startled as the light of the candlesticks illumines faint crimson spots on the floor.

These stains run distinctively through the Holy Place, splattering the curtain, before they finally disappear under the veil. Then the sound of His voice wells up from deep within as He speaks these words: "We have confidence to enter the Holy Place by the blood of Jesus, by a new and living way which He inaugurated for us through the veil, that is, His flesh. Let us draw near with full assurance of faith, having our hearts sprinkled clean from an evil conscience and our bodies washed with pure water." What? A new way by His blood! My conscience sprinkled clean? No more guilt? Free from the past?

Overwhelmed at your discovery, you practically push at the curtain, trying to follow the blood through the veil. You can barely follow the drops illumined by the candles as your eyes fill with tears of inexpressible joy. You mutter to yourself again and again as you try to find your way within the veil, "I'm free, no more guilt! I don't have to carry the guilt of my sin any longer! I am free to fulfill my destiny! There is nothing to hold me back! I can go on in His purposes with nothing to separate me from Him!"

With hands trembling now and knees weak, you think you cannot stand another moment of separation between your Lord and you. Your heart is blazing openly now, almost violent in its abandoned pursuit of Him within the veil. Giving in to your heart's desire, you do not have to look remorsefully at your future any longer.

For the first time, you can see that He is there with you, and there is nothing from yesterday that can hold on to you or divert your attention. Your future is in Him, a future filled with God-initiated, God-directed and God-empowered service. Now every move is effective and every plan confirmed. His Kingdom comes and is established in you and in those around you.

Now, all those "spiritual tools" you brought along to help you in this incredible search are seen for what they really are: cumbersome reminders of times of genuinely believing that you had to earn approval and work for salvation. Although you would never admit it, in your heart of hearts you knew that was your real motivation. Surely God would accept you when you displayed all you had to offer. How wrong you were!

Now, with all these "spiritual tools" securely attached, and your desire for Him peaking, you can take it no longer. Overwhelmed with emotion, you momentarily lose consciousness.

When you awaken, you sense a ferocious pain in your eyes, as though a thousand suns were illumined before you. Everything is quiet. You are all alone...or at least you think you are. The pain in your eyes is so intense that you cover them with both hands. But somehow the light still seems to shine through. "Come, My son," a gentle but firm voice calls to you. "The blood of My firstborn Son has made you clean." Suddenly, His Spirit churns within you and you are drawn to Him. Like the dawning of a hundred new days, understanding begins to flood your heart. "When we see Him, we will be like Him." All at once you become painfully aware of the "tools" you have been carrying.

Through tears of repentance, still lying flat on your face, you begin to take off that which only moments before made you who you thought you were.

Your doctrines are the first to go, thrown at the base of the Mercy Seat. Your talents are then tossed at His feet, quickly followed by your gifts and ministry. It's amazing how these once-sacred crutches have quickly become an anathema to you, since they only separate you from your Lord.

Still flat out, you continue at an almost frantic pace to take off idolatry, financial and career security and political prowess. And just when you thought you were done, you are shocked to realize that all these were external, outward things that were really only hiding more insidious and destructive impulses of the heart. But even these are now becoming visible in this spectacular light.

Now you are shedding personal ambition, greed and lust for position. Bitterness and unforgiveness are quickly pulled off as you cry out to God, "Touch my lips with the burning coal, that I may speak purely and righteously all my days!" Sorrow and grudges, insecurity and unbelief are the last burdens to be shed amid your muffled sobs.

As you lay there before your Lord, breathless and dazed, you sense a cleanness that you have never before experienced. Though exhausted, you are lighter than air. There are no clouds in your sky, nothing to make you run, nothing to make you fear.

You have lost your urge for religious activity and meaningless ritual. There is no longer the driving force of guilt to keep you busy and tired, hopeless and in despair.

You let out a childlike giggle as you sense this unimaginable freedom. Oh, the liberty! Oh, the ecstasy of being found in Him! Your giggle turns into a laugh as joy from the deepest part of your heart wells within you, a joy so deep, so full and so indescribably powerful that it almost frightens you. But yes, you know it's from Heaven and you know it is real.

A second time, the voice of the Father is heard. "My son, the blood of Jesus has been sprinkled to the Mercy Seat. Come up hither!" Without giving it a second thought, you begin to rise. But then bone-chilling, humiliating reality hits you. You are still full of joy, but a bit perplexed, as you consider your seemingly awkward condition. You cannot get up from lying prostrate before the Lord, for you are totally, unequivocally naked! You haven't got a stitch of anything covering you!

"But...but I cannot, my Lord! I cannot approach You! For everything I had, I have discarded because of its utter worthlessness in Your light. I am naked, and I have nothing with which to cover my nakedness!" Without a moment's silence, the commanding voice of the Father is unmistakable as He responds, "Who told you that you were naked?"

For just a moment, you are stunned by Adam's hopeless condition. He too was stuck on the ground with no hope of rising. But there on the floor, just where your face meets the earth, is the scarlet glow of His blood. You know that somehow, somewhere in eternity, God has provided. Although you look naked, you feel naked, somewhere, somehow, in God's almighty economy, you are not naked.

"What would happen if I were to stand up right now and obey Him?" The thought is almost too wild to entertain, yet your heart seems to be giving the commands now. Your mind becomes the somewhat reluctant servant. You think, "I am clean, holy and pure." Your hands begin to push your body to an upright position in utter defiance of your common sense.

But sooner than immediately and more quickly than a moment of time, light from between the cherubim above the Mercy Seat swooshes down with a mighty rushing sound and envelops you in Himself. There you stand, stark and utterly naked by man's evaluation, totally devoid of anything that could give a man honor and influence. But in God, within the veil, you are clothed with His light—His unapproachable light!

"For he who saves his life will lose it; but he who loses his life for My sake will find it." How vain and worthless these trappings are compared to Him who is within the veil! You begin to think of John the Baptist, a broken and humble prophet, a stirring preacher and mighty man of God. Yet he knew his frailty. Oh, how mighty a man was he to confidently lay his ministry and crown before the Lord and declare to all the world, "He must increase, and I must decrease!"

As you stand before Him, wrapped in Him and filled with Him, His light carries you unto Himself. You find yourself with Him on the Mercy Seat as myriads of angels sing with a mighty worship to your God. Amid this eternal worship you can hear your own voice making vows to Him.

"I desire to always stay small before You, my King. By Your grace, I will never exchange Your glorious Presence for outward religious trappings. I will never again allow idolatry to replace Your spectacular nearness. I will never use the gifts and ministry You have so graciously given me to try to purchase Your love and acceptance. For I am nothing, utterly nothing. And these things that I have joyfully given to You today, I never want to see again."

With loving, piercing eyes He turns to you, and you know you are being changed. You know you are being transformed into that which will be eternally pleasing to Him. Then His eyes grow stern and angry. Yes, angry. He turns to the pile of worthless rubble you laid at the foot of the Mercy Seat. With a mighty breath, He stares at that which for so long had separated Him from you. With one violent burst of flame, His anger consumes it all! Oh, what an indescribably wonderful feeling, to see the smoke clear! Not even ashes remain! It is gone. It is all gone! Now nothing will ever be able to separate you from the love of Your Father! You are His.

As you sit with Him on the Seat of Mercy, you become aware that your viewpoint has radically changed. After this most awesome experience, you look out upon humanity from within the veil and you see man as God sees him. Your heart nearly fails you for grief at the unregenerate state of even the most zealous believers.

You cannot believe how little of the Lord most people know, and how little of Him most are content to experience. Their substandard condition is appalling, and your heart reaches out to them in pity and sorrow. The Spirit of prayer wells within. You are about to learn the next secret from the Most Holy Place...the secret of intercessory prayer.

Chapter Four

The Secret of
Intercession

You are stunned almost into utter disbelief, yet you believe. Wrapped in Him, seated upon the Seat of Mercy within the veil, everything is different. Your vision is now that of another realm. This otherworldly perspective leaves you speechless and awestruck.

The depth of man's barrenness is greater than you could ever have imagined. The depth of your own barrenness now reaches its full impact. You begin to see that your best human efforts cannot even be seen from His Seat of Mercy. You worship Him as you understand that only His shed blood has given you access to Him and only His living blood maintains you.

But as you look back through the Holy Place and then the Outer Court into the sea of humanity, your heart compels you to go back and tell them of this most wonderful realm of fellowship with Jesus. But you cannot move. Though your heart compels you, His Presence restrains you. The Lord says to you, "My son, for you there shall no longer be a going back and forth into My Presence. There shall be a flowing, continuous, persistent swelling of My life unto the people for whom you pray."

You can no longer focus on yourself as a point of need. Now you have seen Him and have understood that He holds you in the palm of His hand. In the shadow of His wings you will sing for joy. For the Lord is your Helper; what can man do to you? He knows what you need. He has clothed the lilies, fed the birds of the air and watered the earth by His eternal love. How shall He not do much more for you, who dwell in unapproachable light within the veil?

Now you are compelled by the same love and mercy that moved the Lord Jesus to make His ultimate sacrifice. As you see Him minister to the world from within the veil, you find yourself ministering and interceding before the Father on behalf of the needs you see. You are totally forgetful about yourself, totally consumed in Him.

You ask Him fewer and fewer questions as His life continues to increase in you and your own way continues to decrease. You are a vessel, you see that now; one through whom the Lord Jesus does His work. You are one through whom He flows most freely. You are no longer opinionated, no longer giving advice or questioning His bidding. You are but responding to the Lord, who is ever-increasing in your life.

Thoughts of your own reputation vanish as you respond and pray for those to whom you would never expose yourself. The old resisting voices that have always hindered you and held you back are but a clouded memory. You do the Master's bidding in prayer. The manna is not falling from Heaven anymore, for it is now welling up within your innermost being. You have taken your place as part of the Bread broken so that life may come forth. Compassion constrains you to pray and pray some more. You feel as though you should physically step out and make something happen. But you realize that He does not need your arm of flesh, only your will aligning with His and your spirit submitting to His.

Now your heart, that once beat only *for* Him, is beating *with* Him for His Church and for those who call upon Him for help. You have become a co-laborer with Jesus Christ. You are in sync with His love and in tune with His purposes. Your desires are becoming His desires, your motivation, His motivation and your joy, His joy.

"Come up hither!" you cry out to the Church. "Come up where He is, where there is no striving, but only flourishing life." Your prayers intensify as you cry out, "Come up hither, where there is no more going out of the camp to gather bread for the day. Come to the place where you become one with this eternal Bread, broken yet glorified for His sake and to fulfill His purposes. Come up hither, where there is no more going, but only flowing."

You have discovered the secret of intercession and prayer. You have entered His rest. His life now freely flows through you, a yielded vessel. You do not make lives change; He does. You cannot convince the mind or soften the heart; only He can. You cannot heal the brokenhearted or free the prisoner; only He has that power.

You have become an eternal motivator. You see need, brokenness, heartache and despair. You see pain and suffering. You see the lost masses of humanity teeming with insecurity and hopelessness. Like the prophet of old, you offer yourself with passionate resolve: "Here am I, Lord. Send me." You begin to think His thoughts, dream His dreams, love with His love, heal with His life. You are moved by His emotion, and you minister by His power for His purposes.

So you become smaller and smaller, crying out night and day for God's love to subdue the earth. Like Jesus, you pray again and again, "Thy Kingdom come. Thy will be done on earth as it is in Heaven."

Like one who knows he is personally and utterly cared for, you continue to respond and act, not taking into account what man will think or whether man will approve. You are already approved, and He is bidding you go on. You will not insult your Lord with thoughts about His intention toward you. How could His intention be anything different than what He has just demonstrated to you? How could He forget you as you sit, sharing in His unapproachable light?

Like His eyes, your eyes now go to and fro over the land as you pray and respond, intercede and minister from within the veil. Your life is not your own. It belongs to Him who purchased it with the blood of His Son.

As you become accustomed to His life and to experiencing life from His perspective, you discover a strange absence. Although the Most Holy Place is very active and full of powerful worship and splendor, there seems to be a lack of traditional spiritual warfare activities. Surprised at this, you look around, only to discover that all is in divine order here. There is nothing out of Lordship, nothing rebellious. There is no war, but there is nothing to go to war over. For here is eternal and divine harmony. You are beginning to discover yet another secret, the secret of spiritual warfare.

Chapter Five

The Secret
of Spiritual
Warfare

Calm assurance. Yes, that's the best way to describe the feeling you have as you watch and learn from His perspective. In fact, "calm assurance" is probably a little too weak; it's more like total confidence.

Everyone knows exactly who is in charge here. Everyone knows who protects, covers, guides and gives commands. There is no shouting here, no rampaging enemy about to subdue the army of God. You are in His Domain, in His Covenant, and you are walking on the highway of holiness, where the unclean cannot travel and fools dare not venture.

You are enveloped by His unapproachable light, secure in His Kingship where there is no lion or any vicious beast. This land has become springs of water where the redeemed of the Lord walk and everlasting joy dwells. Passing into the Most Holy Place, you have left dualism behind. Flesh cannot rule within the veil, nor can your enemies pursue you there. Deep within, you hear the prophet's words. "Speak kindly to Jerusalem, and call to her, that her warfare has ended." You see Jesus' victory on the cross in utter totality. The defeat of the enemy was final and complete.

You are dumbfounded at your own naivety as your eyes gaze upon the risen and victorious Christ. Nothing has been left undone. You begin to understand that God is not at war. He has won. You remember the mighty suit of armor you loved to wear and the huge sword that glistened in the night as you waged ferocious warfare on behalf of God's Kingdom. And for the first time since you have been clothed with light, you are ashamed as you remember. This experience—your shame—is one you will repeat again and again as you learn and discover His ways and allow Him to restructure your thoughts and actions according to this new perspective.

No longer bound by a limited theology or the traditions of men, you begin to see a covenant of unleashed splendor, a covenant so totally complete, so perfect in power and love that you know in your heart of hearts that your war is over. Again, with tears of utter joy and gratitude, you fall to your knees in humble worship of Him who has gotten for us the victory.

Suddenly your glistening sword appears on the floor in front of you. With final repentant resolve, you lift the handle with one hand as, grasping a rock with the other, you begin to beat the sword into a plow. With each sounding of rock against metal, you are more determined.

Tears streaming from your eyes, you are recrafting this former weapon of war, and you vow not to do again that which has already been done. You are entering His Covenant, His Domain and His victory. No longer will you be a man of war. No longer do you need a weapon of destruction. No longer are you left to your own abilities to protect yourself and your family.

As this revelation floods your innermost being, you discover a new tool in the making, a tool that will plant and build and cause life to come forth from death. With this new tool, fashioned by your own hands, you are truly entering into the labor of Him who is building, restoring and planting new and abundant life. You are now a part of that life which flourishes from within the veil and covers the earth.

Here God has arisen, and His enemies have scattered. His light has dispelled the darkness. Your puny attempts to shout and scream at demonic forces are no longer needed. In fact, they never were needed. You have heard, in your heart of hearts, that dwelling in the light as He is Light separates you from even the most stubborn demonic force. He must come forth. He must come forth in you, in the Church. But He must come forth. Your shouting does not strike fear in the enemy. Only His Presence strikes the proper fear in the proper place.

It is becoming more and more clear to you. For all your rebuking and fuming and casting out of devils, the world has not changed all that much. You have always known that only a change of heart will ultimately free anyone and that true repentance is the only way to release the work of the New Covenant in a person's life. Nonetheless, you have been bound to externals, leaving the issues of the heart to run wild and rampant within. You have declared freedom to these people, demanded wholeness and claimed prosperity for them, but you have not changed their inner being. Externals have always been more fun to change, since such a "transformation" gives the appearance of happening so quickly.

But you made a costly error. You had forgotten the glory of the New Covenant. When there is true repentance, the inner change is total and permanent. Behavior changes from within, not from without. No wonder Jesus always said that the Kingdom of God was within! In utter disbelief of the time you have wasted and of your inadvertent disregard of the work of the New Covenant, you determine that you will not do again what your Lord has already accomplished.

You have moved beyond the Holy Place, the arena of traditional warfare. You have moved away from duality: from flesh and spirit to Spirit; from God and satan to God, from life and death to life. No, you will never wage war again, but you will plant the seeds of life and enter into the work of the Father.

You labor within the veil, looking over your shoulder as though an enemy were approaching. But he never will. Then you realize the truth: The war is over. Like Israel of old, you are building a habitation of God in the Spirit. But unlike Israel of old, you do not need one hand for building and one hand for holding a weapon. Both hands, your entire being, your entire heart, can be dedicated to building, because the war is over. And this building is without sweat, because it is initiated by God, directed by God and accomplished by God. You will never again cower in fear or look to the future with forboding uncertainty. The war is over.

Like the woman caught in adultery, you are gathered unto Him within the veil as the Lord, your

Lord, powerfully confronts your accusers. In shock and unbelief, you look frantically around to see who or what would accuse you first. Surely there would be someone with brazen hatred or vengeful determination to rail at you. Surely, surely...but all is quiet. You look this way and that, again and again. Finally, with a look of eternal relief and a slight, joyful laugh, you turn to the Lord, saying, "There is none, Lord."

Then the triumphant voice of the Lord responds in glorious melody, "Neither do I accuse you, for the accuser of the brethren has been cast down. He who had continuously badgered with guilt and shame is silenced and you are free." You are just beginning to grasp what the Lord has really been saying to you. "My beloved son, the war is over."

Chapter Six

The Secret
of Rest

othing can ever replace life within the veil! Nothing can replace the humbling clarity of His life. Here you will work less, but accomplish more. Here your busyness subsides, but your effectiveness increases a hundredfold and more as you listen and respond only to that which comes from Him.

You are discovering the utter worthlessness of wood, hay and stubble. You are in shock as you see how these works of man are so barren before the flourishing life of the Father. Your heart wells up within and your voice vows again before your King, "By Your grace I will never again work apart from your work. I will never again draw my own plans and construct my own castles, even in Your Name. I vow to lay this before You, never again to take it up."

The Lord's eyes quickly turn to your fleshly efforts. In less than a wisp of time, they become smoke and are gone. A thrill runs through your heart as you realize that the pain of letting go is really unlocking arenas of life that you never dared even imagine could be freed. Your wasted time can now become quality time. Your wasted creativity can now be given to His glory.

But with an ache of remorse you recall the hours, the days, even the years spent in such consumed busyness. And all for the sake of the Kingdom! For a brief moment you want to protest. For a brief second you want to defend your valiant efforts and the efforts of your friends. You want so badly to tell the Lord that you worked hard and that at least the work kept you in church and out of trouble. You want to explain why you thought this Bible study and that Sunday school project and those other meetings were so important. You want to explain all this, but...you never get the chance.

Instantly the Lord reminds you that your own efforts just went up in a billowy puff of smoke. You stop in mid-thought. For there are no excuses for busyness. There are no excuses for a schedule so full you barely have time for your family, not to mention the Lord. But now you have entered His rest. You have stepped within the veil. You have entered His work, and there is nothing that can compare with the satisfaction and fulfillment of knowing that what you are doing is absolutely as effective as it should be and could be.

You are no longer working for work's sake, no longer working to gain God's approval or to win His favor. You have His favor, and His blood gives you His approval. Now you need only do what He says. Everything else will burn.

You have a confident assurance for the first time in your life. You know you are in Him and you know you are doing His bidding.

Your concern about the opinions of others also fades. While you do not want to offend, how can you stop your own pilgrimage for their sake? You are not haughty, you are not proud. Check your heart! How do you feel at the thought of serving God in such fulness? Does it make you feel as though you are better than others? Do you think you have earned or deserved what you have? Of course not! The answer to these questions is a resounding "No!"

You are broken at the privilege of working in His field and under His command. You are saddened that everyone seems to be working so hard. His load is easy. His burden is light. His service provides the time to adequately care for each responsibility He has given us. There is no help for us as we build on our plans of wood, hay and stubble. His only instruction to us when we are in this mode is to stop doing and listen for His voice.

As you gaze into the realm of humanity, you are saddened at the pace at which the Church is building that which will most certainly burn. Almost oblivious to the voice of the Father, the Church appears to be accelerating its stubble-building at a frantic pace. "Will they ever stop?" you ask the Lord. "Will they ever hear Your gentle call and cease their flurry of activity? Will they ever take a stand against that barrage of demands and requirements on them?"

With a sigh of longing and anticipation, you hear the Lord deep within you. "Deep calls unto deep. They feel what I feel. They sense the longing within them as I do. But they choose not to respond. Some have convinced themselves that they don't hear Me at all. Others have such fear that they ignore Me. Still, there are others who will work and work to cover up their inner longing. But I am greater than their work. Only when they enter into My work will they satisfy their inner longing. For only My work can survive My shaking. Only My work is eternal.

"I am greater than their fear and their pretense. I will not withdraw My heart from them, for how can a

mother forget her nursing child? No, I will continue to call to them and draw them until the aching in their hearts overcomes all their resistance. I have secrets for those who will be drawn away, for those who will come up hither unto Me."

Through tear-filled eyes you recall all your own resistance and the list of excuses you have used. Your heart is broken by the knowledge that He did not have to beckon you, that He is sufficient in Himself. He did not have to draw you and be patient with you. Yet He continued to strive with you until the time that you abandoned all for an eternal relationship with Him.

Busyness does not bring the glory of God, nor is your weariness a sign of spirituality. In fact, the opposite is more probably the case. He knows what you need. He knows what is required to care for you. Is He not able and willing to take care of you? Should you not be spending your time seeking His Kingdom? After all, "all these things will be added to you." Why? Just because He loves you. Not because you have worked yourself to exhaustion.

"Come away, My beloved! Find the joy of resting in the arms of your Father."

Chapter Seven

The Secret
of His Glory

D
ay passes day, week follows week. Deep within is the unshakable knowledge that you have moved through the veil, that you do not come into and depart from His Presence, but you abide with Him. You will not let Him be Lord only sometimes, but you permanently surrender your will to His. No matter how demanding the day, His Spirit continuously witnesses to yours. You are within the veil, in Him and out of your self. You can almost feel yourself change. You recognize that His power is now freely at work in your innermost being, and you are becoming like Him.

Oh, how small you feel! Oh, how unworthy you are! Oh, how will you ever understand the magnitude of a timeless love that transcends your frailty and gently lifts you to His bosom? You do not deserve it.

You do not earn it. But oh, how you love it! You would not trade it for all the gold and silver in the world! You have yielded to Him and now the fulness of the New Covenant is at work within. Concepts once a blur now become more clear. Things that were confusing begin to find their relevance. Spiritual truths that always seemed so elusive are finally beginning to take form.

"Glory" is one of the those concepts you never quite grasped. For all the deep theological definitions you had studied about the word, you seemed as ignorant as ever as to what it really meant. Was it a large white cloud that billowed in the early dawn? Or was it some spiritual "pixie dust" sprinkled over the earth by legions of silent angels at night? Whatever it was, you certainly never dreamed that glory was something real. Not only is it real, but you never imagined that glory was an experience you were destined to play a role in bringing about.

You begin to see God's people all over the earth. Their witness and testimony are convincing people that Jesus is Lord. These are people who genuinely care. They are hearing the Father and are responding to His life within. Some of these are praying, some are feeding the poor. Some are preaching, while others care for runaways. Some hold Bible studies, others operate soup kitchens. There are believers praying for the sick while others care for teenage mothers. None is fulfilling his own desires; each is doing only what God has given him to do. Their work is not in vain, for work initiated from within the veil produces a life that flourishes from the hearts of those who minister. Their lives shine with a light from beyond this realm.

"Oh, how wonderful!" You marvel as you see so many converted. "You are watching My glory at work," you hear the Lord say to your heart. "My glory is that which convinces man that Jesus Christ is Lord."

You begin to understand as you recall that you are being changed, transformed from one degree of glory to another. Glory is simply God's convincing splendor. It convinces the world that God is alive. And that glory fills the earth as it fills you. There is no spiritual pitcher from which He will pour some metaphysical ooze called "glory"! There is nothing otherworldly about it as such. Its otherworldliness lies in its ability to point a physical human to a spiritual God. Glory has the instant result of moving man's heart from his own troubles and the certain doom thereof to the awesome abilities of a compassionate and caring God.

All that takes place through you who are filled with His convincing splendor. You are the lamp through whom the Anointed of God is brought to the four corners of the earth. You will be part of the fulfillment of the ancient prophets' testimony, "As surely as I live, all the earth shall be filled with the glory of the Lord, as the waters cover the sea."

You begin to realize just how much others do watch you! When you glow with peace and joy, even in the midst of difficult circumstances, you convince the world that Jesus is Lord. When others see compassion and mercy growing in your life, they see Jesus. When they see your actions and language changing so completely, they are convinced of His power. When you can hold down a job for the first time in your life, when you begin to really love and respect your spouse, when people see that you are content with what you have and are happy to share with the needy, they see the convincing splendor of the Lord inside you. And it makes them want the same thing you have.

You shake your head in wonder. He never stops amazing you! "All the earth shall be filled with His convincing splendor." "Every knee shall bow and every tongue confess that Jesus Christ is Lord, to the convincing splendor of God." Yes! When the world sees His glory, it is seeing Jesus Christ. And when the world sees Jesus Christ, it is because His convincing splendor is emanating from you.

People will repent when they see Jesus, your Lord, having His glorious will being done in you! When unbelievers see you in selfless, loving obedience to Him and view the remarkable and tangible results of His ruling in you, they will want the same thing you have. They can listen to you talk all day with few lasting results. They can read your books with little effect. They can see you preach for years, yet it will not have the impact of seeing you flourish as Jesus is Lord of your life.

The world craves reality. You know that now. The world is desperately searching for meaning. Even within the "church," the hunger has reached famine proportions. God's people are in a desperate fix. The child is ready to be born, but there is no strength to bring forth. It is a day of trouble and rebuke. Many words are being preached from one end of the earth to the other. Volumes are being recorded.

Yet people are in want. They are starving for words of life. They are waiting to hear the gospel of life, the gospel of His Kingdom. Jesus declared that He is not the God of the dead, but of the living. Reality is the only hope of a condemned world and a bankrupt church. A living God doing eternal work deep in the heart of hurting people is the gospel of life, the gospel of the Kingdom.

There is very little today to convince anyone that God is alive. But He is alive in you! Your spirit burns for Him. Your heart is filled with His glory. Your life is filled with convincing splendor. You have the key within you to once and for all reverse this seemingly irreversible situation.

You stand breathless before the Lord. You had no idea! You did not have a notion of the destiny upon you. You press your hands hard against your chest. You want to believe that you can make a difference. You want to believe that you hold the keys. But somehow you cannot let go.

Suddenly the Lord begins to show you the path you have traveled the past several years. You see what you have always hoped was the case, but never really knew until now. Through all those events of your life, both good and bad, God was there, intimately involved in your life. And He was not only there, He was changing you, preparing you, leading you to repentance and change until today you see yourself as He sees you. You behold yourself as one who is filled with His glory, one who is filled with convincing splendor.

Because what is happening in you is real, many will gravitate to you. You do not need obnoxious religious jargon, nor need you pretend to be spiritual or try to be holy or work at being righteous. His glory shines through you without those exercises in futility. In fact, those carnal attempts at convincing others only backfire and make it more difficult for what is really there to shine out.

He *has* begun a good work in you. "You are His workmanship, created in Christ Jesus for good works." "Greater is He who is in you than he who is in the world." You do not have to pretend. You do not have to fake anything or try to make it happen. Your utter yieldedness to Him is all that's required. This is real. This is convincing splendor. This begins within the veil. This is His glory, and only His glory will change the world.

Chapter Eight

The Secret
of Perfection

very passing moment brings new insight into the ways of God. Because you are in His House, seated on His favorite Seat, you can look around and see His personality everywhere. Misconceptions in your thinking and theology are evident wherever you look. Although this is a bit painful, the exhilaration of knowing the truth and of its setting you free is worth it all. With each new discovery, you are experiencing your Lord more fully and enjoying fellowship with Him with unprecedented satisfaction.

You begin to realize that Israel was chosen of God even while it was in bondage to the Egyptians. You ponder this thought. God's chosen people were under bondage and slavery, even while they were God's special treasure. But their status as the chosen did not bring them to a "deliverance" status. While they were in Egypt, they did not even know the Name of the Lord who had chosen them. After Moses spent forty years in the wilderness and saw God in the burning bush, he still had to ask Him His Name. In Egypt, Israel knew only hardship and oppression. They had no spiritual insight, no fellowship with the Father.

With this new insight, you see that Israel's journey from Egypt to the Promised Land actually parallels your own journey to the Most Holy Place. Egypt was a type of the Outer Court, your initial conversion experience. There, you were washed in the spiritual laver, the blood of Jesus. Your works continued to be intense, since you had no sense of destiny and little sense of being accepted. Just like the Israelites in bondage, who knew little more than brick-making from morning till night, you never knew your God.

But God sent a deliverer to Egypt. Moses, a faithful servant, led God's people out of Egypt and into the wilderness. Here the people began to know God slightly. The wilderness was a place of mixture. Flesh and spirit fought it out here. But here God would begin to show Himself to His people. This is a type of the Holy Place, where the candlesticks of humanity burned with the oil of the Holy Spirit, producing light. The wilderness was a place of occasional supernatural intervention. It was a place of the partial, where you "look through a mirror darkly."

How well you can relate to that! How well you remember the frustration of not having the answers for so many people. You remember, with pain and sorrow, how you prayed and prayed, but sometimes there was no assurance that He heard. Your heart wells up with gratefulness as you realize that time has passed and a new day has dawned in your heart.

The Holy Place was also the place where man discovered the degenerate greediness of his flesh, for he is never satisfied. No matter what the Father provided in the wilderness, complaints, murmurings and unbelief were soon to follow. Life in the wilderness was not an exciting experience. God never intended that Israel, or you, do any more than merely pass through this realm to the fulness of His provision.

In his unbelief, however, man found a way to survive in the wilderness with barely a thought of moving on to the Promised Land, though he always wanted to return to Egypt. Although the bondage was gone, the people of Israel were still bound within. They could only relate to that which would satisfy them for the moment. The miracles came and went. The Pillar of Fire and the Pillar of Smoke burned in the camp, but not in their hearts. The manna, the quail and the rock that followed provided for the outward man. The inner man, however, still craved union. The Spirit of God continued to lead them and to work in their hearts until they came to the place of rest, the Promised Land, the Most Holy Place.

Here is the secret. Here is the end of mixture and the beginning of His fulness. Whoever believes enters the rest. With solemn confidence you know that it is not the strong, not the rich, not the talented who enter His rest, but those who believe. These externals, or any others, are of no value in establishing and entering into fellowship with God within the veil.

Now you know that your resting place is within the veil, not in Heaven. It is for now, not then. Within the veil there is no sweat, no trying to attain what is already yours, for you see as you are seen, you understand as you are understood. Continuing to yield to Him, you come to know that God is calling you by His Spirit into a realm of Christianity that is far beyond your wildest imaginings. This will not be an outward flamboyant display of the miraculous. It will not be a man-centered gospel of personal kingdom-building. It will not be a gathering unto a group or a stream or an organization.

Within the veil, where only His light shines, there will be a gathering unto Jesus. Believers will walk in solid inner strength and assurance as never before. You begin to realize that His Name really is written on your forehead and His laws truly are inscribed on your heart.

The Sabbath is also a type of the Most Holy Place. Its fulfillment is not a day, but a condition of life. The meeting of the saints can occur any day, as long as they meet. But the Sabbath is special, it is holy, because it is the posture of your relationship with Jesus.

You are set aside for the Lord. You please Him because of His blood, and there is absolutely nothing else you can do to make yourself more pleasing to Him. Your striving is over, your war is over and your struggling is over. You are accepted in the Beloved. Your consciously making an end to all striving demonstrates to Him that you believe. It is at this point, where you purposefully stop working for approval and realize that you are approved, that you truly become a believer. You always thought acceptance and approval were so elusive, but your abandoned, almost reckless (by human standards) refusal to be ruled by the flesh demonstrates that you believe His blood is sufficient.

You now begin to see your service to Him in a wonderful light. Your service is not to gain or attain or win. Your service is because you have already attained and you are co-laboring with Him. It is a result of relationship to Jesus and not the means of gaining a relationship. It is not a means of eternal life, but a joyful entering into His labor because you have eternal life.

You see, you have just discovered a monumental secret. Perfection is not a behavior: Perfection is a relationship. Perfection was never intended to be measured by how you behave, but by a relationship; a personal, abiding fellowship with the living Lord, Jesus Christ. When perfection flows from relationship, there is a liberating desire to please the One you love. Your heart soars with the anticipation of responding to love. Your fear of sinning and your poor self-concept begin to fade as you mature in this newfound fellowship.

What keeps a marriage intact, but a solid relationship? What determines the behavior between husband and wife, but a desire to be pleasing to one another? In a love relationship such as this, who is concerned with falling? Who is concerned with what not to do? Love motivates. Love creates. Love gives expression to itself in a manner that increases the intensity of a love that already exists.

Love produces loving actions. Loving actions produces more love. The cycle goes on and on. Where is there time to fail here? Where is there time to go astray? It seems apparent that one is perfected in love. It seems that a genuine love relationship moves behavior to a higher plane of expression. This expression is no longer based on a list of dos and don'ts. It is not based on a code of ethics or a moral law. Love has lifted you beyond that realm. The law no longer restricts you, because your love constrains you and motivates you and encourages you.

Apart from this relationship, your life is reduced to legalistic bondage. There is no love to inspire, to create, to bring joy. When there is no relationship, you do not really know what pleases Him and you cannot experience His Spirit bearing witness with your spirit that you are His son. This leaves such a void that all your guilt and fleshly attempts at gaining His approval have preeminence in your life. You are working. You are trying to be good so you can go to Heaven. Constantly you try to do the things that you hoped would let you stay in His favor. So you pass out more tracts, join the choir, pray more, memorize more Scripture verses, and on and on.

And because there is no relationship, you always seem to fall short of God's standards. Instead of doing all these things as an expression of utter joy and gladness, they become a hopeless exercise of tediously trying to gain God's approval which, of course, you already have because of the blood of Jesus.

With this kind of starting point, the issue becomes the unattainable: "Be ye perfect." Perfection is never the motivator, never the underlying issue, for unconditional love can never hold such lofty standards over a humanity that can never, in itself, be perfect.

Your only hope is to step into Christ. Your only hope is to believe the gospel and fall hopelessly in love with Him who redeemed you at the cost of His own life. For when relationship is at the center, genuine perfection will not be far behind.

Chapter Nine

The Secret
of Our
Inheritance

—

Mow long do you suppose you would
be satisfied to be engaged to be married, but never actually marry?

That's a rather strange question, isn't it? Nonetheless, the Lord clearly is requiring an answer to this
most unusual query. Your thoughts go back to your
own engagement. The anticipation was such a thrill!
The feeling of soon being married to the one you
loved so desperately was one you would never,
ever forget. "But how long," the Lord interrupts
your thoughts, "would that excitement remain if the
wedding day were never known and, worse, never
arrived?"

"I suppose," you respond hesitantly, "that it would
get quite wearisome after awhile. After all, you don't
get engaged to be engaged. You get engaged to get
married. The engagement is only a temporary condition until the wedding can occur." The light of the

glory of God in the face of Jesus brightens as you begin to see a neglected truth of the New Covenant.

* * * * * *

A man comes to your home, a lawyer from a distant land. He has come on a surprising mission. It seems that your great-uncle has died. In his last will and testament, he has left you the bulk of his rather massive estate. This visitor from a distant land speaks of legalities and details that you understand little, if at all. Finally, he assures you that the inheritance will be delivered to you.

As your mind reels with shock and incredulity, you try to decide whether or not to believe him. He looks authentic enough. Sounds true. And you do remember something about a great-uncle living in a distant land somewhere.

But just as logic is about to dismiss this gentleman as an evil and terrible prankster, he pulls a leather folder from his briefcase. Yes, it is a folder. As he unties its ends, he assures you that this small token, this down payment, is merely to confirm to you that the rest is indeed on its way. The folder unravels onto the floor with a thud.

To your amazement, more money than you have ever seen falls to the floor. You pick up one of the many bills and say to yourself, "I did not even know they made bills so large." The lawyer leaves you a card and walks out as you sit dumbfounded at the awesome wealth that lays before you. The attorney opens the door again, briefly poking his head back inside. "Remember, this is only the down payment, the guarantee. The full inheritance is to follow."

* * * * * *

The young bride-to-be was radiant. She was beside herself with joy. With the giddiness of a teenager, she called all her friends. She wanted everyone to see her ring! It was such a lovely ring. It seemed almost to shimmer in competition with the radiance on the young woman's face. "Isn't it beautiful?" she exclaimed as she proudly held out her left hand for all to see. She was greeted with smiles and eagerness to hear all about the man who would soon be her bridegroom. She had waited for so long. Now she had her guarantee! They would be husband and wife!

If there were not so much genuiness in her excitement and admiration in her heart, one might almost say that she was a bit obnoxious about the whole thing. After all, how many times can you look at a ring? How many ways can it shine in the sun? But such an event comes only once in a person's life, so her friends let her enjoy it to the fullest.

* * * * * *

You still cannot believe what this lawyer has done! You are sitting in the middle of what probably is more money than you have ever seen in your life, maybe more money than you have ever imagined. Certainly more than you ever thought would be yours in your entire lifetime. With great excitement you begin to tell family and friends about what has happened. "Isn't it wonderful?" you gasp in unbelief. Your friends are so happy for you! They know you so well. They know how hard you've always worked. So what if you got a little irritating as you shared your good fortune? After all, it is not every day that such a wonderful inheritance comes to someone. Your friends understand, so just enjoy! It's a once-in-a-lifetime occurrence.

* * * * * *

Dawn comes, the rays of the sun piercing the diamond mounted so beautifully. The stone casts a soft bright light upon the bed, where its recipient is wiping away early morning tears. As she watches it sparkle in the sun, her grief overcomes her once again. "What good is a ring when there is to be no wedding?" she thinks. How hollow the promises of that ring seem today.

She quickly rolls over in the bed so her back is turned toward it. Even to look at it brings too much pain. Even to remember how she so confidently displayed her ring brings an unbearable ache to her heart. How could he have let her down? How could he have promised so much, yet fulfilled nothing? How would she ever be able to face her friends and family again?

They would never understand. They could not understand how or why she could have been so thoroughly deceived. She was not normally so gullible...but the ring, oh, that ring! It had taken away all doubt and seemed to prove to her that his intentions were genuine. But now she feels so empty. Yes, empty, and sorry and confused. She just wants to sleep her grief away and to forget this horrible, horrible time of utter dissappointment.

* * * * * *

With every dollar you spend, you begin to wonder when the full inheritance will arrive. Certainly the down payment was more money than you have ever seen. However, it was not more money than you could spend, for there is need all around you. Countless people have been helped by this down payment so far. Not only are the needs of your own family finally taken care of, but the needs of families and individuals across the land are being met by your hand of generosity. "Freely I have received," you heartily say, "and freely shall I give!"

Unfortunately, though, the giving must soon come to an end if the fulness of the inheritance does not soon come through. Your thoughts dwell upon this more often now. You fumble through all the papers on your desk until you come up with the card the lawyer gave you. You try to make contact, but he is never in. He never returns your inquiry. And he never comes back. It makes no sense, but he never returned. How or why would someone leave such an incredible down payment as a cruel joke? It is something you would never understand.

One day, you hear a knock at the door. A messenger dutifully hands you a telegram. Immediately you recognize it as coming from the attorney. With your heart racing, you pull the envelope apart. "Dear Sir: It has come to my attention that you have been calling my office repeatedly. I am sure I made it clear that the full inheritance will come. I even gave you a down payment to prove it. Please let this matter be settled. The inheritance is yours. As to its delivery date, I shall follow the directions given in the will. Upon your death, I am to deliver the remainder to your home." End telegram.

* * * * * *

A long time ago believers fell into a serious bad habit. Whenever they did not understand something, or whenever they did not experience what the Bible said they should, they simply developed a theology that made room for their shortcomings. Soon, more and more of these precious promises were experienced and understood by fewer and fewer people. Over the centuries, an incredible thing happened. The Millennium became the Golden Age of Christendom. The Millennium was when everything wonderful would happen. This life turned into an almost unbearable drudgery as you waited for that great someday over there.

But you have heard all of this already! You should be going on to other things. True, but do you realize that almost all of the work of the New Covenant has been assigned either to Heaven or to the Millennium? It seems there is precious little you and I can do beyond hanging on until the end. The fact is, in some people's theology, there is not much more grace than that available anyway. It has gotten to the point that this life has been robbed almost completely of the glorious provision that is ours in this New Covenant.

Can you believe how naive you have been? You actually accepted as fact the idea that the Holy Spirit, as a down payment, was to carry you until you die. Then you would get the full inheritance. Think about it. What good is an inheritance if you are dead? Who dies to inherit a great estate? The one who leaves the inheritance is the one who dies, not the one receiving it. An inheritance is a living memorial granted by one who has died. Though our Lord rose again, His death passes the inheritance on. For centuries, grown men have been wanting to die to inherit the promises of God. They have been waiting to die to experience the fulness of their salvation.

While the Lord is revealing these truths to your heart, resistance mounts. Contesting voices clamor to be heard, voices that come from pride, religion and established theology. Remember, old traditions do not die so easily. Old, favored doctrines do not so simply pass away. They will be heard, but they will not prevail. So the questions come.

"Don't you believe in Heaven anymore?" "Don't you believe in the Millennium?" "You mean you think you can be perfect in this life?" "You believe everyone should be healed?" Oh, have you heard these questions before—and a thousand just like them! You could spend hours carefully answering each inquiry, painstakingly detailing that you do believe the Word. The other alternative is to recognize a smokescreen when you see one. Do not let these questions ever sidetrack you. They are designed to shock you into thinking you are dealing with borderline heresy. If these distracting voices can scare you by questions you cannot answer, then those who resist going on are free from conviction. Hopefully you will not be sidetracked.

But you know better! You have experienced life within the veil, beyond your will. You know there is more! You have experienced the pain of a betrothal with no marriage. You have used the same lame excuses again and again as to why you did not experience what the Bible seemed to offer. You know what it is like to show off that ring month after month, year after year, yet still have no wedding. You have discovered that the joy is in fulfillment, not in excuses. The real peace is in experience, not in a futuristic theology.

You have seen Him! You know the inheritance is for here and for now. It is becoming more and more clear that Jesus always dealt with the issues of this life. His main focus was His Kingdom coming to earth. He was not preoccupied with Heaven. His Lordship is for now, not for then. You see that man must stop pushing God's purposes into the future. Man cannot so easily free himself of the responsibility that he carries before God for his own generation.

God is looking to and fro across the land. He is looking for people like you. He is looking for you because you are willing to bear the yoke. You are willing to carry the responsibility that He has for you.

You are willing to examine the New Covenant again, to scrutinize its contents and to test its interpretation over the centuries. He is looking for a people just like you: willing to say yes to Him and to the purposes of God for your generation.

You have seen the transitory realm of engagement. That ring is only for a season! There is a deeper intimacy waiting for you that you cannot even begin to imagine on this side of the veil. The ring says that invitation is real. Soon, instead of showing the ring, you are clothed with the Groom, and you are becoming more and more like Him with each passing moment. Union was never intended for death! Union is for now! How simple. How freeing!

Tears of joy stream down your face as you find yourself experiencing an utter abandonment to His desire for you! With an ecstasy beyond words you yield to His gentle invitation: "Come unto Me, all you who are weary and heavy-laden, and I will give you rest. Take My yoke upon you and learn from Me. For My yoke is easy and My burden is light." With total delight you comprehend. Union with God requires death. But not physical death. Instead, you must die to your will, rend your heart and go through the veil of your stubborn will in this life. This is genuine union.

Now an awesome thing is happening. You see Jesus walking toward you, glowing with the joy of simply being with you. As He approaches you He becomes transparent. Through Him, in all its speechless and unutterable splendor, you glimpse eternity. Spectacular rays of brilliant light shine through Him. You can hear Him laugh as you peer through with childlike wonder.

There are vast expanses of His love waiting to be experienced. Valleys are a plush green, spangled with the brilliance of a thousand colors of flowers you know are not of this earth. Rivers running deep and teeming with life invite you to enter. The sound is as though all nature is singing a chorus of such resplendent contentment that it seems the universe is dancing with joy.

You have discovered that you were never intended to make it through on the down payment alone! The Holy Place is to be passed through on your journey to the Most Holy Place. The day requires more than you have had. The forces and powers of the last days can only be confronted by that which is within the veil. Our hope of victory, as well as our hope for unlimited power, find their source in the One who is unlimited within the veil.

Eternity, once so elusive, has come near. Eternity, once kept at a distance, once thought to be a future experience only, is now available to you through and because of your Lord. With His compliments, He invites you explore the vastness, the depth, the wealth, the intimacy and the love He has purchased for you within the veil of the Most Holy Place. Within this veil, you will discover the fulness of the New Covenant.

Chapter Ten

The Secret
of His
Sovereignty

You are stunned. You are afraid. You cannot believe what is happening before you. But it is true. This drama really is taking place in earth, in Heaven, in God. He is a Rock. He is a solid Rock, and He will not budge. He simply will not move. You watch, transfixed. You do not understand. To be sure, you are not even certain you want to be witnessing this.

You see a man, an older man, lying on a bed of affliction. Doctors, nurses, specialists and other very important-looking people in white gowns and masks scurry about his bedside. Bottles drip unknown liquids directly into his veins. Electrodes are attached to his head and chest as someone carefully monitors sophisticated diagnostic equipment.

Yet with all this activity in the room, there are almost no words. The only sounds are those of clanging surgical instruments, an occasional rush of oxygen and the continual gurgling of intravenous medication. There appears to be almost no hope among those so dutifully tending to their responsibilities. It is almost as though they already know the inevitable is about to happen.

You look across the way into a large church building. There you hear what should be a beautiful and encouraging sound. For there, men and women have come together to pray and intercede. You soon understand that they are praying for the man you have just seen in the hospital. You hear their cries and listen intently to their prayers as they try to move God to bring healing to the man. You want to join them in their petition. You want to reach to the grief and sorrow that they feel, for you feel their burden. You feel their pain.

But as you attempt to join in their chorus before the Father, you sense the hand of the Lord sternly restraining your participation. You turn to the Lord, questioning His leading. His eyes pierce yours with love and resolve. You cannot comprehend why, but you know that God will not be moved. Immediately you realize that the man will most definitely die. For God is as solid as a rock on this one. He will not be moved.

Back in the hospital, the team of physicians slowly moves away from the bedside. One pulls his mask off in sorrow, shaking his head as he goes. You hear the slapping of surgical gloves as another pulls them recklessly off his hands and tosses them to the floor. Only one person remains at the bedside.

Carefully the electrodes are removed from the man's head. The needles are retracted from his arms and tossed onto a tray. For a moment, she stops to look at the man. Finally, with a sigh, she slowly pulls the sheet over the man's body and covers his head. She slowly turns and leaves the room, turning out the light and closing the door as she goes.

The desperate prayers continue unabated at the church. But God won't be moved. One by one grand Scriptures are shouted Heavenward. " 'By His stripes we are healed.' You promised!" you hear one say. "Your Word demands a response—'If you ask anything in My Name, I will do it!' " another cries out.

You turn to the Lord, to find Him filled with grief. For hours He has been attempting to reach this little prayer meeting. He has wanted to minister to these people and give them direction. But they had already mistaken their grief for the Spirit of God. They had already determined that their anger was God's boldness and their frustration was His resolve. So they continued throughout the night. But God would not be moved. What He had determined could not be changed. For He is God, and sometimes God cannot be moved.

As dawn breaks and a single ray of sun passes through a corner of a huge stained-glass window, the door of the church opens slowly to reveal the broken and sobbing messenger of certain bad news. He stands there silently. The rays of early dawn begin to shine in more freely now, flooding the altar area with a bitter false hope. The shock moves quickly through each person. The messenger says not a word. But his silence delivers the news with a cruel eloquence.

In one final move of utter desperation, someone jumps to his feet and shouts, "Thus says the Lord, 'Do not believe what you see, for I am God! I can raise even the dead!' " But God cannot be moved. He is God. "Thus says the Lord, 'Do not stop praying, do not stop believing!' " Grief gobbles the man's remaining efforts as he slumps to the floor in disbelief. But God cannot be moved. The hollowness of this desperation adds a kind of sinister mockery to the already shattered gathering.

One by one, the people slowly walk toward the door. The only sound is that of a Bible being thrown to the floor. Another person quickly places his guitar into its case and snaps it shut.

One person remains at the altar. She carefully puts the lid on the anointing oil. She reverently gathers the bread and wine of a communion service that took place sometime during the night. Before she leaves, she turns to the large wooden cross behind the altar. Without a word, with a solitary tear falling from her cheek, she turns and slowly walks away, turning off the light and closing the door as she leaves. God is God. Sometimes, God cannot be moved.

In a glorious flurry of light and with innumerable angelic beings, the man's spirit is whisked away to the Presence of the Lord. Thus will he always be with Him.

You want to ask the Lord, "Why?" You want to know. You feel for the people. You mourn their loss. The pain in your heart is real pain, your tears are real tears. You need an answer. Certainly, it was not as though He did not hear the prayers. It was not as though He was distracted, for He was intently watching the people and deliberately determined not to respond to them.

Tears flow more freely down your face now and you shake your head in utter disbelief. He did not move. He was absolutely not moved by their prayers. To be sure, He was affected by their prayers. For anyone could see the distress and sorrow He had for those praying.

But certainly there was no good reason to let the man die! Certainly, with all God's wisdom and all God's power He could have spared this life and fixed whatever needed to be fixed, either in the man or in the circumstances or in Heaven. Certainly He could have made room for this life to continue. Look at his friends, how they weep! Look how they loved him.

You turn to your Lord, the One who holds the keys of hell and of death, the One who bought you by His own blood. You turn to Him for an answer and instead are confronted with perhaps the most bittersweet of His secrets thus far. God is God. He is a Rock. And sometimes He will not be moved. Sometimes the answer to our prayers is "No."

"And no, My son," the Father responds before you ask, "No. I will not tell even you. I will not disclose My purpose to you or to anyone else in this man's life. I am God."

Suddenly, all your emotions and all your questions, frustration and confusion come crashing to the surface. "Have you betrayed me, my Lord? Was all that I have suffered in vain?" Again the tears stream from your eyes. As you sob uncontrollably, your mind races wildly. Betrayal, lies, deceptions! "What was His purpose? Why will He not give me clarity? What have I done to deserve this kind of treatment?" You have given all to Him. You trust Him. You rely on His wisdom!

You are angry and bitter. As far as you are concerned, you are wholly justified. You deserve an answer! But...but...you finally see that, just like those praying in the church, you were demanding out of your own grief. Your anger made you bold and you defiantly confronted Him who was pierced through for your iniquities. Like these "prayer warriors," you have mistaken your frustration for resolve, gaining a false sense of self-righteousness as you dare trample His courts with your fleshly rantings. He who was bruised for your iniquities and chastised for your well-being is misunderstood as mere mortal man sends forth arrogant taunts from his finite understanding and mortal existence.

Your Lord's eyes are dark and stern as they slowly turn to you. His countenance is hard and His voice like thunder. "Where were you when I set the stars in their places? Where were you when I spangled the darkness with their brilliance? Did I ask you to advise Me as I set the sun in its place and the moon to guard the night? Did you counsel Me as to how I should place the mountains or plant the valleys with their elegance?"

He walks toward you, and a tear falls from His eye. He opens wide His arms as He says, "Where were you when I dropped to My knees at the side of that river bank, when I gently and lovingly formed the man with My own hands out of the dust of the earth?"

And through eyes blurred with emotion, you hear Him ask, "And where were you when I gently bent over this lifeless form, my lips touching lips of cold, course sand, breathing into them the breath of life, that man might become a living soul?"

You collapse to your knees and fall headlong before Him who led captivity captive, crying out in fresh repentance. "Jacob I loved," the Lord continues, as though He did not hear you, "but Esau I hated. And who are you, O man, to answer back to God?"

You hear your lips forming words of worship. "You are God. Sometimes God will not be moved. God will not be moved." Quickly you begin to comprehend His sovereignty. To co-labor with Him means you enter His labor: He does not enter yours. You pray according to His will and intentions, not according to your own personal plans or understanding. You cannot lean on your own understanding. It will always get in the way of His will. The carnal mind cannot alone comprehend a spiritual God.

God is a Rock. He will not be moved. You see a secret: If you want your prayers answered, you must pray the prayers He wants to be prayed. If you want a miracle, do what He is doing. If you do not know what He is doing, go into your prayer closet and close the door. If you do not have direction, you do not go. If He gives you nothing to say, you are silent on the matter.

Your opinion is not what matters. His will is all that counts. If, perchance, God gives you a choice, He will tell you even that. Your confession will, from now on, be that of Jesus Himself: "I only do what I see My Father in Heaven doing"…nothing else.

Before God, you resolve not to let emotions, even strong emotions and passions, replace the genuine leading of God. You resolve to stay still and small so you can accurately discern and divide between soul and spirit, even between bone and marrow.

In front of you is a huge Rock. He is the Rock of our salvation, and He cannot be moved. You cast your frustration against this Rock and it is dashed to pieces. Your anger and self-righteousness are next to fall against the Rock.

Your rights, your grudges, your self-justified anger have kept you from Him. Because you thought you knew better, you let walls of bitterness grow between you and Him who is the Door to the Most Holy Place. Your fleshly demands to know have hindered the blessings due you because of the Covenant He cut with you when He poured out His life's blood in your stead. This confusion, though pushed deep within, has caused you to stumble. You know now that your balance can never be recovered until you let go.

"I submit my will to Yours. You do not owe me an explanation. I owe You repentance. You do not have to explain anything. By Your grace, I joyfully embrace Your will."

Though the grief is intense within you, a very deep inner pain is fading away. Though your sorrow is indescribable, you are being released into a new dimension of trust in God. He is God. Sometimes, He cannot be moved.

There are times when His purposes transcend your human ability to understand. But thank God for those times! Do you want to be able to bend God's will and twist His arm so that He gives you what you want, instead of what is best for you? Thank God that sometimes even our rantings over misunderstood promises and selfishly applied Scriptures cannot move Him. Thank God that He cannot be backed into a corner or be turned into a waiter who responds quickly and obediently to our every beck and call.

You realize that He is God. In the last analysis, you must, in humility and love, submit your will to His, yield your plans to His and back off so His purposes have preeminence. For God is solid as a Rock. And sometimes, God cannot be moved.

Chapter Eleven

The Secret
of Relationship

There is no place, no use and no need for a formula within the veil. There are no carnal concoctions of a feeble humanity that force God to do or be anything at all. He is God. And He is moved by only one thing: genuine love. He is touched beyond measure and moved beyond imagination by a heart that has fallen desperately in love with Him.

From your vantage point of relationship, you see that yet a deeper relationship is possible. From your posture of humble worship, you see His determined resolve for you to be real with Him. Yes, even to be comfortable in His Presence. With singular clarity you understand that He really does know how many hairs are on your head. He does know your coming and your going. Before you can even voice a word of praise or prayer or worship, He has already received it in His heart. He saw you being formed in your mother's womb. There is absolutely nothing hidden from Him.

He knows you. He knows the good, the bad and the things you try to hide. You only get nervous around Him because you don't know that He knows. But He does! All those things you always meant to tell Him, those few hidden problems that in your heart of hearts you realized He would need to know...He knows! Remember, He has seen you naked. He has seen you in all your frailty. You don't have to be ashamed anymore, for He has seen you as you really are and has clothed you with Himself in unapproachable light.

So, yes, you can be comfortable in His Presence. His concern is for the heart. When your heart is after God, your heart will bring you to purity. He is appalled by externals! He is disgusted with your meager cover-ups. He does not want His courts to be trampled by men and women whose hearts are cold, but who externally produce a show of humility and personal commitment. God has never been and absolutely never will be satisfied by any external display of piety or religious activity.

You hear the word of the Lord welling up within you, carrying all the power of eternity. His voice shakes with exasperated authority as He sees men and women attempting to approach Him on their own terms. In such awesome intensity His voice thunders in your heart.

"What are your multiplied sacrifices to Me? I have had enough of burnt offerings of rams and of fatted calves. I take no pleasure in the blood of bulls, lambs or goats. Bring Me these worthless externals no longer. Even your incense is a stench to My nostrils. I can no longer endure your external displays! Rend your hearts and not your clothes! Circumcise your hearts and not your bodies, that there might be holiness from your innermost being and righteousness pouring forth from your lips!"

Oh, how you see man's depravity! Oh, how you see his concoctions, his convincings, his ruthless attempts at deceiving the living God. Oh, how you understand His mercy! When man extends his vile arm of flesh to move God, he deserves nothing less than destruction! Your lips pour forth prayers of repentance for yourself and your brethren. You can hear yourself crying out for mercy at the blindness of man concerning God's ways.

With a deep inner chill you discover that God does not wink at sin. He does not ignore it. You discover that the blood of Jesus which cleanses sin does not make it any less visible to Him with whom we have to do. Just because you are forgiven does not mean He is not pained. It doesn't mean He does not notice. Oh, the blood of Jesus! Oh, the blood that washes! Oh, the blood that does more! It gives you power over sin!

You see Him and you are becoming like Him. You are no longer content merely to have your sins forgiven. You are no longer happy just to say your sins are covered. For you have seen Him! You have seen humanity's sin before Him and you are ashamed. Denomination after denomination passes before you, doctrine after doctrine flashes in front of you. Argument after argument, self-righteous platitude after self-righteous platitude fills your mind and spirit, and you cry out with desperate realization, "There is none righteous, no, not even one!"

You are horrified at the totally futile arguments that divide. You are appalled at the puny excuses for sin that we offer the Lord. These external fig leaves only expose man's nakedness. You are again stunned that it was Adam's attempt to cover himself that exposed his nakedness. The fig leaves only drew attention to those areas of nakedness he tried to cover. Man is naked. He is naked. He is naked, and no amount of external, carnal embellishment will ever change that. God is looking for the heart. He always knew Adam was naked; He knows you are, too, apart from Himself.

The Kingdom of God does not come with signs to be observed. You can fool men, but you will never fool Him. You cannot clothe yourself with signs. Miracles do not cover you. Ministry does not cover you. Big churches can never cover you. Only Jesus can cover you.

The Kingdom of God is never eating and drinking. It is never that which covers the outside. His Kingdom is a matter of heart. It has always been a matter of heart. It has always been that which proceeds from within. His Kingdom comes to you as you allow Him to etch His laws upon your heart. When your obedience is complete, born of desire, His Kingdom has come to you. Externally enforced laws may keep you out of trouble, but they will never, ever bring you into His Kingdom.

You find yourself vowing before the Lord never to allow an external to interfere with your relationship with Him or with a brother or sister in Christ. You see that a right heart will be taught of the Lord. A person in right relationship with God and intimate fellowship with Him will be led into all truth.

In the distant recesses of your heart, you begin to hear walls coming down. Their crashing gives you a feeling of exhilaration and joy. You know your heart yearns for Him. That is your touch point of relationship. You are also seeing that others, maybe many others, whom you have excluded over the years also have a heart for the Lord. This now becomes your point of fellowship. You have nothing to hide anymore, nothing to defend, nothing to prove. This is your point of acceptance. Now you never want to sin again. You cry out to God for strength and mercy. "Help me, Lord! I never want to offend You again."

You sense the comforting Presence of the Lord enveloping you as He draws you to His bosom. "Grant that I might live purely all my days," you pray quietly. He is about to answer your prayers. For you are soon to learn the next secret of the Most Holy Place, the secret of total salvation.

Chapter Twelve

The Secret
of Salvation

"**O**, that the salvation of the Lord would come out of Zion!" The intercessory prayer grows more intense as you see from His view. "O, that the fulness of the New Covenant would be manifested through God's people!"

You have been content with the partial for so long. You have been content in your minimal experience for so many years that you have adapted quite well to its utter deficiency. Your doctrines have changed to accommodate it. You have forced many wonderful New Covenant provisions into that indefinable dimension called the Millennium. But that has all changed now.

From His view, life apart from the fulness of the New Covenant provision is not possible. You desperately need all that Jesus purchased for you. Your spirit groans with emotions too deep for words. The flighty quoting of Scriptures and the flippant recital of a positional doctrine in Christ will no longer suffice. To win—and God does want you to win—there must be a total fulfillment of the New Covenant deep within your heart. His first appearing, as your Sin-Bearer and Healer, brought you to this point. But now you need more; you need Him if you are to win.

Again you abandon your heart to His will and eagerly look toward His full manifestation. He is not going to bear sin again. He is going to be bearing the salvation of the Lord, a dimension beyond the veil, an experience of the third day, a relationship that will transcend both gifts and abilities. This encounter will cause your heart to overflow with His love and mercy. As His strength wells up within you, your voice rises above the clamor of subtle confusion and inner tyranny.

"I can do all things through Christ who strengthens me." Though you have heard this verse a thousand times before, only now does it deposit inner fortitude and resolve into the very center of your being. Previously you had only mouthed the words; today you are experiencing them. "I can do all things through Christ who is my Strength. Through Him I can run through a troop and leap over a wall."

And in the course of it all, you will never even come to a sweat, for it is not you who must labor. It is He who accomplishes His work within you.

You understand more fully than ever now. You are not healed for your sake alone. You are not delivered only for your own well-being. Jesus has redeemed you, healed you and delivered you, that you might be a yielded vessel through whom He might minister the fulness of His salvation to the earth.

He has set the prisoners free. He is binding up the brokenhearted. His Presence is comforting all those who mourn. He is pouring out His joy and the oil of gladness upon His people, that they might be the planting of the Lord, trees of righteousness, bearing fruit in every season and constantly bearing green leaves upon their branches, leaves that will heal the nations.

And He gives all this, not just for your sake, not just so the Church can close herself off from the rest of humanity, spending a lifetime pouring the same water into each other's vessels; not so she can maintain a level of wholeness or shield herself from the hurting millions who need bread to eat, water to drink, health to be restored and hope to plant. For it is you who will restore what the canker worm and palmer worm have eaten. It is you who will restore the old waste places.

Yes, even in your brokenness—in fact, only in your brokenness—do your hands drip with His oil, and your cup overflow with His living water. You will restore the ancient ruins. You will recover the people lost to generations of desolation. One word from your lips will deliver a man unto the Kingdom of His beloved Son. You will reclaim what enemy has claimed. You will deliver to the Lord what past generations have let disintegrate. Your hands, your words, your acts of love, oozing with His Presence, shall restore a generation to the Lord. With untold joy, you realize that it is not too late to experience the fulness of your salvation.

Yes, it is clear now. Very clear. You were never called to sit. You were called to minister from within the veil. You were called to be redeemed and to redeem. Your life now is to flourish with His life. How could you have missed it? To be converted merely to maintain and hold on until the end was never His intention.

You have only begun to experience the fullest measure of the New Covenant. You have only begun to touch the rest of the New Covenant reality. No longer will you be part of a whimpering, impoverished and frightened church. No longer will you cower in the corner, hoping for Jesus to come and rescue you out of your troubles. No longer is your hope merely in Heaven. It is now in Him who indwells you with might and power.

Now you know that He did not bring you out this far just to let you go back again. His deliverance is complete. To spend the rest of your days where you have been would be like the children of Israel never entering the Promised Land. The desire of God's heart was never only to deliver Israel from Egypt! His intention was twofold: to bring them out of Egypt and into Canaan, out of bondage and into the land flowing with milk and honey.

Oh, how you have tried to maintain a life so far below His salvation! How you have ignored the second part of God's provision! He never intended that you merely be delivered from sin and its terrible bondage. But He will not give up until you have stepped into the Promised Land, where real intimacy begins and His life subdues yours.

Within the veil, this total salvation begins to manifest. Now everything does not look as it once looked. The Church takes on a new dimension. Here, seeing the Church from His view, it looks vastly different. In fact, you are dumbstruck at the abruptness with which your vision has changed. You are about to discover the next secret of the Most Holy Place...the secret of the Church.

Chapter Thirteen

The Secret
of the Church

You have never seen a storm such as this one in all your life! The blackened night is periodically splattered with light as lightning streaks from one part of the sky to another. Angry, rolling thunderheads batter the earth with torrents of water. Hail and sleet can be seen shimmering through the darkness with each flash of light. The guttural sound of thunder seems almost to shake your soul as it growls across the landscape. Nature seems to know it must submit to such thunderous scowls. The trees bow and bend low before the piercing wind and relentless rain. On and on it goes.

You desperately scan the horizon; there is no sign of the storm's ending. How you hope to see a distant sliver of orange gold just above the peak of the eastern mountains! But no such relief is there. The maelstrom is continuous. It would almost be monotonous if it were not for the fear and uncertainty it wrought in your heart.

In the midst of this angry barrage of nature's fury, men can be seen frantically attempting to erect some sort of structure, some sort of protection from the storm. With each flash of light, you begin to notice that there are hundreds, maybe thousands of people huddled together around these buildings. The relentless wind drives the icy rain against them as they shiver with cold and gloom.

Families stand together, some entwined in blankets and others holding tiny children inside their drenched coats. Occasional whimpers and cries from frightened toddlers are quickly tended to, although little can be done to improve their lot. No one moves. You see only blank stares as they watch the men labor hopelessly against the storm.

Your heart begins to shiver as you wonder what this vision might mean. You have already seen many marvelous, even glorious things since you stepped within the veil. But this is different. Somehow, you are sure you will not like what you are about to see.

The dull blackness begins to give way to a sullen gray as dawn approaches. The storm has not let up, even for an instant. The rain and ice, driven by the wind, continue to angrily pummel both the workers and those watching. The fog, moving swiftly along the ground, lends a ghostly appearance to this hopeless scene. Forms of many more people become visible in the early dawn.

But something very perplexing is happening. In the night, when vision was limited to the streaks of lightning, you had a very different thought as to what was happening. You thought there were maybe twenty or thirty men working together in their attempt to build a shelter. Almost in disbelief, you discover that what you saw was not twenty or thirty men frantically working, but twenty or thirty or fifty different work sites.

These men are not working together! They are not even talking from work site to work site, even though the buildings are so close as almost to be touching. Not only are these men not working together, site to site, but there appears to be quite a level of disorder within each work area.

The storm has made communication so difficult that few are even trying. Work is done in a haphazard, even helter-skelter, fashion, all in an unfruitful effort to build a shelter. You even observe one group building one side of a wall and another group, only a few feet away, tearing down the same wall.

119

Each seems to be convinced in what he is doing, yet little is really being accomplished. Each seems to have his own plan to follow, almost oblivious to what others are doing. In exasperation, you turn to the Lord. "Wouldn't these men benefit from at least trying to understand what the others are doing?" But the vision continues as though He did not hear you.

The morning brightens, if you can call it brightening; the clouds continue to roll low in the sky, spewing their anger upon the earth. Other, even more bothersome sights become visible. Why, some builders are pulling at those watching, occasionally snatching one or two here and one or two there, forcing them not only to work on the structure, but to become part of its walls.

Ruthlessly they pound and bend, trying to get these poor folks to fit into slots of the builders' choosing. Often in the course of building, these people are tossed aside in disgust, not being able to be correctly fit into place. Sometimes stones and blocks are discarded as well. These are hurled haphazardly into the crowd, where some people are hurt, maimed and even killed by the flying debris.

"What is happening?" you cry out to the Lord. "Is there no one to really help these people? Is there no one with answers?" In frustration, you burst out to

God, "Where is the Church in this time of crisis?" Immediately the answer comes, piercing and streaming, and quite unacceptable to your conscious mind.

"You are watching the Church," the Lord replies. "Or what man has called the church over the centuries. Instead of this world's storms driving them to Me and to one another, their pride and stubborn hearts drive them to a self-determination that destroys not only themselves, but all those they are so sure they are called to love and shepherd.

"Men who have no time to wait upon the Lord build according to the partial illumination of the candlesticks in the Holy Place. Worse, they may build according to old patterns, left in the past because their time was done. They can never discern the depths of God on this level. They can never see clearly concerning the Church in the Holy Place. The light is just not there."

But what does this mean? Why have you worked so hard? Why have you struggled so long? To be sure, there are those few who have labored to provide a safe harbor for God's people. There have been those for whom the veil was pulled back, and Jesus truly displayed His Lordship upon them. Yes, here and there genuine church life is experienced by those who have no reputation to defend, no agenda to put into place, no other motive than His love. But even though you try to contain your human emotion, you almost cannot help being angry. You have accepted a definition of the Church of Jesus Christ that is vastly different from the one He said He would build.

"I am quite sorry I must do this," you hear the Lord speak gently to your heart. "But if you are to understand, you must know the truth. Anything that you build that is not from within the veil is not the Church. Did I not say that I would build My Church, and the gates of hell would not prevail against it? Pardon Me if I tell you that that Church is not for the Millennium. It is not for some future generation to have to deal with. This Church is part of My Covenant provision for you.

"Do not be alarmed if I tell you that those churches that hurt, inflict pain and impose legalism and guilt are not built by Me. Churches in which members revel in adultery, slander or gossip were not built by Me. Any place where wolves are permitted to devour the sheep is not My handiwork. The Church I am building is built of broken hearts who are willing to be changed by My power and consequently can yield to My power. These people will be as abundant as the dew in the morning. My Church does not stand idly by, watching their brethren be deceived by religious charlatans who milk and rob My people of the money that should be used for My purposes.

"My Church is a haven from the storm. It is a place of rest and strength. The Church I am building is a Church strong in love and compassion. There is a highway in this Church—the highway of holiness. The unclean cannot walk its pavement, for it is for the redeemed of the Lord. They will walk this highway free from the oppression and bondage of men. There will be none to devour in this Church, no lion lurking to tear asunder the people of God. There I Myself will shepherd My people Israel. There I will gather My people to Myself. And the tug of the Spirit will be stronger than any wall you might be able to erect.

"I will draw My people to this Church. Walls of prejudice and envy will come crashing down as men and women of broken and contrite heart respond quickly and with resolve to Me within the veil. For this is My resting place forever. Here will I dwell. For I have chosen Zion, I have desired it for My habitation. I will abundantly bless her provision; I will satisfy her poor with bread. I will cloth her priests with salvation, and her saints will shout for joy."

You begin to understand the weariness of the Lord with all your petty excuses and lame attempts to set aside this glorious Church for some future day. Yes! Your heart leaps with exhilaration—it is possible! Jesus does want to build His Church here and now, a Church that even hell cannot affect.

How strange it now is to hear a pastor proclaim that his church was ravaged by the devil. His group might have been ravaged. But if it were truly His Church, it could not have been touched. This is not good news for the carnal. It is not good news for those who have been diligently building in the storm, with no direction, no unction and no help.

Beautiful structures of wood, hay and stubble have been erected for centuries in His Name. But just as in the vision, they cannot protect and shield from the storm, for they are not of Him.

But let us be patient. He is determined. He will build His Church, but it will be built within the veil, by broken and contrite vessels who have no agenda and no desire for glory. We are about to see His Church emerge, the virgin Church, who has not bowed the knee to Baal and has not lain with Babylon and its wickedness. When we see this Church come, she will be awesome in beauty and splendor, strong in character and purpose, and desperately in love with Jesus.

Chapter Fourteen

The Secret
of the Veil

Without question, the most elusive, even the most frustrating, part of this journey is the veil. It stands with little explanation and precious few clues as to its place and function in the Lord's eternal plan.

So you inquire of the Lord as you are seated with Him on the Seat of Mercy within the veil. Together with the Lord Jesus, you can look out through the torn veil. As you peer through the Holy Place and see the masses of people beyond the Outer Court, the Lord brings to memory an earlier experience. He reminds you of the day you were clothed with unapproachable light as He drew you unto Himself, to the Mercy Seat, for the first time.

You perceive that He is going to take you through that same experience again. This time, the Spirit of revelation will unveil much more of what actually took place that glorious day when you stepped through the veil and were clothed with unapproachable light.

You recall that as you were walking around the Temple, you were desperately searching for an answer. You cannot quite remember what the driving force was at the moment, but you do remember the depth of pain and the desperate urgency with which you searched. As you explore the Outer Court, the realm of all things that are natural and have an end, you find no answer.

This Outer Court, within the Temple but far from God, offers little beyond a cleansing of sorts. Not a natural cleansing, of course, but a spiritual cleansing. There is no help here from within the veil. Other than this cleansing from sin, you are left to your own wit and wisdom in living your life and discerning the best course of action in various circumstances.

Here, in the Outer Court, people gather in untold numbers. It is a safe enough realm; at least it is within the Temple compound and away from the general turbulent existence that is the normal way of life apart from God. But in this flesh realm, where all things pass away, there is no accountability, no sense of destiny and no desire for either.

Those who sense destiny and accountability do not stay long in this shallow area of religious experience. Those are the ones who are compelled to look further. They are not content with a cleansing, but they want to be changed. They want to be holy. They want to serve Him. Not at all least, they simply want Him. Just as you do! And just like you, *need* is often the driving force that consumes all others. You want to be all these things that you know will please Him. But you cannot. Flesh and blood cannot inherit His Kingdom.

"But who wants to live his life with flesh and blood?" you ask yourself. "Who is satisfied with this?" With that question, you resolve to continue your journey, your search for help...your search for Him.

Moving into the Holy Place, you discern that something momentous has just happened. You have not merely moved from one room to another. You have stepped into a whole new realm, a realm not limited to flesh and to the natural course of things. You have stepped into an area where the Spirit of the Lord permeates everything you are, everything you do, everything you think. This is an exhilarating realm. Every place you look seems to be flourishing with life. You sense His nearness as you never thought it was possible to experience Him.

In this realm, not of the natural, not of the body, but of the soul, His Spirit bears witness with your spirit. For the first time, you know that you know that you know that you are His. Here you experience His help and His leading. Here the Presence of Jesus Christ is real! He heals your body. He heals your soul. His Presence comforts you. His Spirit does miracles for you and those who are close to you. He speaks to you and encourages you. He is with you all the time. Even when you wake in the night, you sense His nearness. It is His delight to show Himself to you. It is His delight to answer your prayers.

In this realm, two-way fellowship with Him can be a daily experience. In the Outer Court, the natural realm, this kind of fellowship is unheard of. There, man only responds to mechanical and repetitious doctrines of religion which only serve to disguise the relationship that is possible in the Holy Place.

But even in the midst of this reality and excitement, even in the Presence of God, even with the miracles that seem to happen one right after the other, there is a quiet agitation. All is not as it seems here. All is not as idyllic as one would think it to be. For though His Presence is so real, and though His Spirit witnesses to yours, the Holy Place is the realm of dualism. In the Outer Court was flesh only, but in this realm, the realm of the soul, dwells both flesh and spirit.

And, oh, the conflict flesh and spirit cause! Since the flesh is at enmity with the spirit, there is never peace. The struggle is constant. Here, the relentless temptations of the flesh try desperately to distract your spirit from the real joy of your heart. The sense of His Presence comes and goes. In this realm, where war between flesh and spirit is constant and deadly, emotions run very high and very low. Strong assurance often mixes with condemnation and confusion. Your sense of disappointment and frustration are only temporary, though, for you realize that these feelings drive you to a greater resolve to find Him more fully.

You recall that it was your search for Him that drew you to the Outer Court to begin with. It was your compelling desire for Him that kept you dissatisfied with that natural realm. Deep within, you recognize that same restlessness overcoming you again. It is not at all that you are ungrateful, but this duality is not what your heart yearns for.

You have said many times that you need an answer. Now, after all this time in the Holy Place, you realize that the answer you are looking for is really Him. You begin to understand that the answer is not a tidbit of knowledge that will merely satisfy your curiosity. The answer is Jesus Christ Himself, in whom are all the hidden treasures of wisdom and knowledge.

Your inner dissatisfaction puts you in a dilemma. The Outer Court, the natural realm where all things come to an end, did not, could not, give you satisfaction. It did not have the answers you needed. That frustration drove you past the laver into the Holy Place, the realm of soul and spirit. There you experienced Him for the first time and understood His love for you in a brand new way. But flesh was still there, sin was still ever so present. You experienced a level of power that you never before realized existed; but you still fell short. You still lacked something.

You almost felt like a bull wandering about in a shop of fine china and elegant crystal. You knew that sin was not to rule you anymore. But sometimes it did. You tried to walk the straight and narrow aisles of rules and laws. But you always seemed to knock something over. You wanted to do everything that Jesus asked you to do, but somehow you always found a reason to avoid His directions. You hated it, but somehow it continued anyway! In this realm, you thought love would be easy and compassion would come naturally. Here you never realized the struggle and resistance that would still be part of your life.

As you ponder these thoughts, you realize that you can never be satisfied with life until all your resistance, all your rebuttals and all your rebellion are gone. You will have to move on.

As you approach the veil of the Most Holy Place, your heart begins to beat wildly for Him. You know that only He can deliver you from yourself. Only He can change you from deep within. You cannot change yourself. You cannot make yourself obey or submit. In an instant, you see the crimson spots on the floor. Immediately, you realize that those spots are drops of His precious blood. You follow them and sigh ruefully as they disappear under the veil. You want Him, you want to be clothed with Him so desperately. Tears fill your eyes as you lean against the veil and cry out to Him.

Suddenly, a thought pierces your mind; with jolting pain it echos deep within your spirit. You fall to your knees, longingly and lovingly touching a drop of His blood ever so tenderly with the tips of your fingers. "He had to die." Shaking with reality, you say again, "Jesus had to die. He had to give up His will for His Father's will. He had to embrace His destiny even though it would cost Him His life." Deep in your heart, you now know that if you really want that depth of relationship, it is going to cost you your life as well.

This is your answer. This is what you were waiting for. You want Him. Oh, how you want to please Him and be found blameless in Him! Like that old, clumsy bull in the glass shop, you remember your actions and reactions of the Holy Place. You recall those times when gossip ruled you. You remember your anger, your manipulations. You are ashamed to remember your uncontrollable rage, your pouting, your lies and your selfish reactions and self-centered lifestyle. You bury your head in your hands as you recall your judgmental attitudes and your merciless actions. You must die to let Him live. To please Him in every respect, you must die to all these self-centered mindsets that keep you from Him.

Still on your knees, you bow down low with tears of utter repentance. "Be Lord of my life. I repent of such horrible selfishness as displays of fleshly ranting. I repent of ruling my own life and resisting Your destiny for me. Never let me usurp Your authority, but may You always teach me how to act and react in every circumstance."

Your heart is broken in sorrow as heavy sobs pour from your heart. "Be Lord. Rule and reign, take over the throne of my life, O Lord." The pain in your heart is piercing and unbearable. Suddenly you hear a loud and merciless ripping deep within your being. As your consciousness fades, the voice of the Lord can be heard in the distance: "Tear your heart and not your garments, that you may be wholly Mine."

As you awaken moments later, your eyes meet the pain of the shining of a thousand suns. You recall how you removed all those things that gave you popularity and fame, respect and prestige. You can still remember the ecstasy of being clothed with un-approachable light and being drawn to the Mercy Seat with Jesus Christ Himself.

But now you know what has happened. He has become, not just your Savior of the Outer Court, not just your Healer and Restorer of the Holy Place, but He has broken through the veil of your flesh, of your own will, and has become Lord. He has passed through the veil of your will and He has taken His seat on the throne of your heart. For wherever He rules, there is His throne.

You have relinquished your right to rule your own life. You have abdicated your throne to Him. He now rules in your stead. He is King of kings. He is your King. He is Lord of lords. He is your Lord. The veil of your heart was torn in two from top to bottom. Now, in the deepest part of your spirit, He has established His throne.

As you see the shambles you had made of things when you were on the throne, and understand how opposed your fleshly will has been to His purposes, you quickly step down from the throne of your life, utterly disgusted by what you had made it. You ask Him to take control. You ask Him to rule over you. You ask Him to be your Lord. You will be content to allow Him to have the throne. You will be content to sit at His feet, to worship Him and to allow Him to do with you whatever He pleases. Now you understand. His blood was sprinkled all the way to the throne. Your throne. He made the way for total redemption. Body, soul and spirit were provided for. In His greatness, in His mercy, you are redeemed.

Here, at the feet of your Lord, you begin to understand the power of God's love. Only His love could compel you to move on. Only His love, causing your heart to throb for Him, could compel you to abandon your will to His.

But the Lord is not going to leave you at His feet. He wraps you with Himself and brings you back to the throne. You cannot believe it. You cannot comprehend it. "Lord!" you gasp. "Lord, I cannot rule my life. Look what a mess I made of it! Have You forgotten? Do You not remember my rebellion? How can You call me back again?"

With a gentle assurance, and half a smile, the Lord responds, "A broken and contrite heart is My delight. He who has torn the veil of his own will has learned an invaluable lesson. He has opened the floodgates of eternal love. My thoughts are above your thoughts, and My ways are above yours. You know that now. You have realized it and have committed yourself to my Lordship."

"But why," you begin to interrupt; but He continues as though you hadn't. "I am a living and loving God. I am not interested in mindless, obedient bodies to serve Me. I need your past. I need your experience. I have led you these past years to train and instruct you. They were valuable years. They were important years. What I have taught you over the years has prepared you for your destiny.

"Now that you have submitted your will to My will, We can begin to rule and reign together. We may begin our eternity together right now. So come up hither. Come up and join Me on the throne that you abdicated to Me. You are a different person now. Your motives are changed. Your hopes and dreams have changed. Your reactions have changed.

"Come up hither, that We may be seated together in this most heavenly place, ruling and reigning together for the Father's glory and according to His will. For it is certainly His good pleasure to bless you with every spiritual gift. It is your destiny. You have stepped through the veil and His preeminence rules. Now the kingdom of your life has become part of the Kingdom of God and of His Christ. This Kingdom, once ruled by you, shall be under My Lordship for ever and ever."

You have experienced the Outer Court, the natural realm, and all it could offer. You moved into the Holy Place, a place of flesh and spirit. There, too, you experienced all there was to experience. Now you have torn your heart, the will of your life broken before Him.

The adventure that is to carry you through eternity begins. Just as the fulness of the Outer Court was only the beginning of life within the Holy Place, so the fulness of the Holy Place is only the beginning of all you can experience from the Seat of Mercy, with Him within the veil of your heart.

But you simply cannot imagine how it could get any better than it was in the Holy Place with the burning candlesticks. Certainly you want it to be better, but how can it be? You are about to discover a brand new secret of the Most Holy Place...the secret of His love.

Chapter Fifteen

The Secret
of God's Love

You have discovered the power of your own will, the power of your own flesh. It is almost inconceivable, but it is true. The power of your own driving will is greater than the power of the laws of God. His laws cannot subdue your flesh. His laws cannot keep you in check. It does not matter how desperately you want to obey His laws. They will never have the ability to make your rampant flesh life submit.

If you want to please Him, if you want to walk in holiness and purity, you must find a power greater than your flesh and greater than the law. You must find God's love in all its fulness and majesty. Only His love has power over sin. Only His love has the strength to draw you away from all that is not pleasing to Him.

So here you fall desperately in love with Him. His love now compels you. His love controls you. His love causes you to walk away from the flesh. You will no longer wrestle against flesh: you will turn and walk away from it, into His love, into His fulness. Here, with Him, you are transformed by this love, and sin's stranglehold on you is once and for all broken. You can be faithful to Him and you will be faithful to Him. You are not a sinner struggling for divine approval. You are a son, washed in His blood and victorious because of His great love for you.

The same love that keeps you faithful to your spouse, the same love that keeps you wholly devoted to that special person, is the love that keeps you faithful and devoted to your Lord. You are determined to annihilate that ungodly doctrine that says you must always sin and you must always fall short. You only fell short until you found Jesus. Did God send His Son so we could continue to fall short of His glory? Did He send His Son to die so that we could continue to be unfaithful to Him? You think not.

The New Covenant provision is more than adequate in its ability both to cleanse and to maintain our hearts in purity before Him. The power of His love is released through the New Covenant. This love compels you to be holy. It is out of this intense desire to please Him that His love has the power to break sin's hold on you. You never again have to muscle your way out of sin's horrible clutches. His love sets you free. His love keeps you free. His love is fully manifested within the veil.

Through your brokenness, through the veil of your flesh, genuine devotion and commitment are demonstrated by loving and pure behavior. Could it really be any other way? You cannot imagine it now. Knowing what you now know, you cannot imagine being satisfied with sin, even if there were a doctrine to support it. To think you actually believed that kind of lifestyle was acceptable!

You begin to imagine what it would be like if this were a doctrine for the marriage relationship. You cannot fathom saying to your spouse, "Honey, you know how much I love you. You know that I am committed to you, but I cannot be faithful. I simply cannot be true. I will love you, serve you, be your friend. I will do all I can to make you happy, but I cannot be faithful. It is not in my nature."

You shudder at the response you would get! Yet you said these words to your Lord when you believed that you could not be faithful to Him! From this perspective, you can understand how absurd that doctrine really is. You can be faithful! You can keep yourself wholly for Him. But you can only do it through His love, the sole force in the universe stronger than your will or your fleshly desires.

You determine that you will continue to yield to Him, to fall in love with Him. Your prayer is that His love will ultimately be the total, compelling force in your life; that His love will permeate your thoughts, actions, hopes and dreams. For it is His love that will finally have the power to bring your destiny to pass.

Chapter Sixteen

The Secret
of His
Appearing

"**A**m I really experiencing this?" you say to yourself one day. "Is this depth of relationship really possible?" You have often heard of those who talked about the deeper Christian life, and you wondered if it were truly possible to experience such a life on this side of eternity. But here you are, enjoying an intimacy and depth of fellowship with the Lord that heretofore you had only dreamed of.

You have taken that step of abandonment. You have given all. You have stepped into Him, and it is wonderful. You can almost feel yourself changing as you see Him moment by moment. You never dreamed that there were so many wonderful things He wanted you to know. You recall with amazement a promise He made to you not very long ago. "The secret of the Lord is for those who fear Him, and He will make them know His covenant." And what a covenant! How powerful! How far beyond anything our human minds could conceive or understand!

Now you are consumed with the burning, almost painful desire to love Him even more completely. "More than anything, I want to know You. More important to me than anything material is my desire to know You." Your most sincere prayers bring quick response from a Lord who delights in showing Himself to His people.

But are you sure you are ready for Him to pull back the curtain of eternity just a little, that you may truly see things as they really are? For things as they are in God are not always as they are perceived by man. Nonetheless, there is nothing that compels you more than your desire to know Him and to see Him.

The one question that you were always positive you would ask the Lord, given the opportunity and right circumstances of course, now seems so unnecessary, so out of place. It is not at all that you no longer care when His Second Coming will be; it is simply that there is now more than His Second Coming to consider. Yes, there will be a literal Second Advent; but you are beginning to understand that the burden of responsibility is not on Him as much as it rests upon each generation.

Each generation is responsible for His appearing in that generation. He has a master plan. Each generation holds an awesome responsibility in that plan. Each must fulfill that for which they were born. Each generation must accomplish what God has determined in His heart for them to accomplish. How easy we made it on ourselves! How clearly you see it now. Oh, how simple to merely look for a physical Second Coming off in the distant future! But what a burden we have put on our posterity. We have pointed to tomorrow, to some future generation, and demanded from them a level of faith and revelation we have not been willing to find for ourselves.

"What about today?" you ask yourself. "What *about* today?" you hear the Lord return the question. "Are you willing," He continues, "to consider for today that which you and your fathers have relegated to the future?" Suddenly, it dawns on you that Jesus preached that the Kingdom of God was at hand. John the Baptist preached the same message before Him. "I AM that I AM" the voice of the Lord thunders in your heart. "I am not the God of the dead, but of the living. *Today* if you hear My voice, do not harden your heart!"

You are beginning to see just how terribly irresponsible the Church has been throughout the centuries. How many promises have we neglected? How much of the New Covenant has been carelessly pushed into some elusive time period called the Millennium just because it was neither experienced nor understood by the Church at large? How much of God's intention for your generation do you quickly dismiss because a man said it was for another place and another time?

The challenge becomes too great. You cannot contain the shock of what you have just seen. "Lord! Lord!" you cry out. "Do not let me breathe my last breath until I have accomplished all that is on Your heart for me! I love Your appearing! But I love Your appearing most fully when You appear in me."

As you look back over the centuries, it becomes clear that God had a destiny for each generation. The purposes of some ages were more visible than others; some were more obedient than others. But at each revelation, at each appearing, carnal men took His precious secrets and hoarded them as though they were their own. As men were greedy for gain, His Covenant became a commodity to be merchandized to the world. Instead of becoming the Body of Jesus, sharing, growing, helping one another and encouraging one another, men began to buy and sell their little tidbits of truth as though theirs were the final words on His character and Person.

Instead of each generation gathering together to fast and pray, humbly seeking the Father, they have retreated behind walls of doctrine and self-righteousness, each raising high his own banner of truth and excellence. Outwardly portraying unity and brotherhood, all the while their hearts have lusted after the loftiest positions. Instead of a standard of righteousness that could have established and reinforced His Kingdom in each generation, men have gathered their dollars and built their own little kingdoms.

At a glance all these little worlds sound like Him. Some even look like Him. There are one or two that try to act like Him. But on much closer examination, they are seen to be whitewashed tombs, devoid of life and possessing only the hollow sounds of a barren relationship and a bankrupt kingdom.

Chills run up your spine and you shudder at these thoughts. But your spirit bears witness with God's Spirit. Your spirit burns with His as He shares with you these awesome secrets.

Now you know. Now you are responsible. Now there can be no excuses. Now there can be no turning back. Each generation is responsible for His appearing in their generation. Each generation. Each generation. As it sinks into your spirit, you find yourself confessing, "My generation, my generation, my generation."

Oh, the purpose! Oh, the destiny! Oh, the burden He's given to us! No wonder He says to you, "Go into your closet and shut the door!" No wonder He continually calls you to Himself! There is a destiny on your generation. There is something wrapped up in the heart of God Almighty that He has set aside for your generation to do.

You are not renouncing past generations or their truths. To be sure, your destiny is wrapped in building upon what they have already done. Your destiny will add to their work as the next generations' will add to yours. But be sure you understand this. If you do not handle His appearing to your generation, but choose merely to live on what has been, it will taste worse than yesterday's manna.

Do not be intimidated by those who will try to convince you that you have nothing to add. These are carnal men who oppose the genuine life of God, the growth that is yours because of Jesus Christ. They write big, important-looking books and bind them with expensive bindings. Even the appearance of these books can be intimidating, as they are intended to be. By the size of their books these men are telling you that what they have is final. But you know better. You know that truth is progressive. You know that every time you see Jesus you are changed a little more into His likeness and image.

So do not respond to these men, but respond to Him who is waiting to appear to your generation. He is waiting to appear to you. He is waiting to show you His Covenant. So respond to Him. Give in to His tugging on your heart.

Go into your closet, and shut the door.

Postlude

So your spirit burns to know the ways of God. Your desire drives you to know the very secrets of God. I was right, was I not? I knew you. I knew your heart yearns for Him. My spirit burns like that too.

The ultimate pleasure in life is to know God's plan, to hear His voice and to walk into all that He has destined for us to become. All other goals fade in the blaze of this desire. All other aspirations are insignificant by comparison.

"The secret of the Lord is for those who fear Him, and He will make them know His covenant" (Ps. 25:14).

You and I need to make a commitment together. We need to have a mutual resolve in light of our new discoveries. Are you ready?

You and I are finished comparing ourselves with other Christians. You and I are finished measuring our faith, our doctrines and our dreams by other men. That feels right, doesn't it? We both have dwindling interests in our needs, our reputation and our fears. We are through trying to fulfill fleshly expectations and treading lightly upon the binding traditions of man. Remember, our hearts yearn for God, for the living God, and we resolve to find Him in an abandoned search for His fulness.

We have barely begun to understand the full provision of the New Covenant, let alone walk in it. We have barely begun to taste the goodness of the Lord that is ours through salvation in Jesus Christ. We have only tasted the fruit of genuine sonship; we have barely understood the passion with which our heavenly Father reaches out to us, or the love so intense that He gave His only Son.

There, we did it. Exhilarating, isn't it? We have made some decisions that will change us forever...just as He has always desired.

This book was intended to reveal some simple, yet powerful, secrets of the New Covenant that are ours within the veil, where He rules as Lord and King in His manifest Presence. If you are willing to step beyond the walls of traditionalism, even Charismatic

Exciting titles
by Don Nori

THE POWER OF BROKENNESS
Accepting Brokenness is a must for becoming a true vessel of the Lord, and is a stepping-stone to revival in our hearts, our homes, and our churches. Brokenness alone brings us to the wonderful revelation of how deep and great our Lord's mercy really is. Join this companion who leads us through the darkest of nights. Discover the *Power of Brokenness*.
ISBN 1-56043-178-4 $9.99p

THE ANGEL AND THE JUDGMENT
Few understand the power of our judgments—or the aftermath of the words we speak in thoughtless, emotional pain. In this powerful story about a preacher and an angel, you'll see how the heavens respond and how the earth is changed by the words we utter in secret.
ISBN 1-56043-154-7 $10.99p

HOW TO FIND GOD'S LOVE
Here is a heartwarming story about three people who tell their stories of tragedy, fear, and disease, and how God showed them His love in a real way.
ISBN 0-914903-28-4 $5.99p
Also available in Spanish.
ISBN 1-56043-024-9 $5.99p

HIS MANIFEST PRESENCE
This is a passionate look at God's desire for a people with whom He can have intimate fellowship. Not simply a book on worship, it faces our triumphs as well as our sorrows in relation to God's plan for a dwelling place that is splendid in holiness and love.
ISBN 0-914903-48-9 $8.99p
Also available in Spanish.
ISBN 1-56043-079-6 $8.99p

Available at your local Christian bookstore.

Internet: http://www.reapernet.com

Postlude

traditionalism, you will find yourself stepping into a deeper realm of His Presence and a more excellent fellowship with God.

His Spirit within compels us to come deeper, to move past the familiar into a reality of supernatural love and power that is beyond our imagination. He is about to visit the earth once again, and He will do it as He is pleased to reveal Himself in you and me. He is about to unveil the fulness of His salvation to those who genuinely fear Him and long for His appearing.

I know you are one of those people.

Your heart gives you away.